MW00460256

Ammo Grrrll Is A Sti

Volume 5   2018-19

ISBN: 978-1-7337313-5-5

Other books by Susan Vass include:
> *Ammo Grrrll Hits The Target (Volume 1)*
> *Ammo Grrrll Aims True (Volume 2)*
> *Ammo Grrrll Returns Fire (Volume 3)*
> *Ammo Grrrll Home On The Range (Volume 4)*

Other books published by VWAM, LLC include these novels By Max
Cossack:
> *Khaybar, Minnesota*
> *Zarah's Fire*
> *Simple Grifts: A Comedy of Social Justice*

DEDICATION:

To my comedic heroes – in standup: Bob Newhart, The Smothers Brothers, Minnie Pearl, Jerry Seinfeld, Ellen DeGeneres, Louie Anderson, Brian Regan, and the late great Wild Bill Bauer.

In print: Mark Twain, Dave Barry and Donald E. Westlake.

In television: Jack Benny.

In song-writing: Brad Paisley, Jimmy Buffett, and Toby Keith.

Profound and eternal gratitude to one and all for the hundreds of hours of laughs you have given me. Without the lot of you, I would probably have lost my mind years ago and been confined to a mental hospital, if mental hospitals still existed. So, I guess I would have just been living on the streets of San Francisco in a modest tent at the corner of Typhus and Poop-fest. Bless you all for keeping me mostly-sane in a difficult and depressing world.

THANKS ALSO BE TO:

The many faithful commenters and fans of my column, *Thoughts from the Ammo Line*, featured every Friday on the center-right on-line opinion site Power Line. These commenters are really now too numerous to mention by name. You know who you are and I love you all.

Special thanks as always to the Four Horsemen Helping Stave Off the Apocalypse with that site: Paul Mirengoff, John Hinderaker, Steve Hayward, and my excellent editor and friend, Scott Johnson.

WHO THE HECK IS AMMO GRRRLL AND WHY SHOULD I CARE HOW SHE SHOOTS?

Since this is my fifth book, frankly I am tired of explaining how I came to be called Ammo Grrrll. I wrote this explanation for Book 4, *Ammo Grrrll Is Home On The Range*, and I think it is definitive. And so, I am just plagiarizing my ownself for this incarnation and maybe all subsequent ones. If you read it last year, and remember it, you have my deep respect.

Here it is: After several decades as a standup comic, I retired and moved permanently -- from Minnesota – where I had to go away for several months in the frigid winter -- to Arizona, where I have to go away for several months in the hellish summer. Sadly, in this great and good land, if you happen to find a place with pleasant year-round weather, you can't possibly afford to actually live there.

Joe (Max Cossack – who writes novels which can be located and ordered on Amazon – did I mention that?) took up target shooting with a nice Springfield Armory .40 caliber pistol. At first, he could just go down to the local Walmart and buy boxes of ammo right off the shelves. But then Barack Hussein Obama became President and suddenly, ammo just dried up. I'm sure it was mostly a coincidence and had nothing to do with the bizarre idea that the Department of Agriculture, to name just one government agency, should have its own SWAT Team and millions of rounds of ammo. Whatever. He's gone now; and at this writing, Donald J. Trump is President and the shelves are once more full of ammo in nice organized stacks.

With ammo in short supply, it became my task to stand in line for many hours a day to secure it. This became a Sacred Quest and a social event and I acquired the nickname "Ammo Grrrll" from the sales people and other customers in line. This continued for a couple of years. Eventually, in March of 2014, I wrote what was a moderately-amusing little column about my experiences in gun-friendly Arizona and fired it off to Scott Johnson, of Power Line to see if he might be interested in a featured piece about the topic every once in a while.

Before I could even go get another cup of coffee, it appeared on the site and -- just like that! -- I was a columnist! It looked like I was never going to have to "Learn to Code" after all! True, there was no money in it, but, fortunately, my husband (Max Cossack, the famous novelist), had already Learned to Code and had done pretty well with it.

I could afford to be a Kept Woman, if you count doing cooking, cleanup, laundry, shopping, and housekeeping for about half a century being "Kept". Having two jobs with the column provides a kind of safety valve for my legendary and professional-level Powers of Procrastination.

When I am "supposed" to be writing, I can decide that it is urgent to organize my sock drawer; and when I am "supposed" to be making and freezing appetizers for an upcoming cocktail party, I can tell myself that I better sit down at my computer and write a topical piece about the 29th Democrat candidate for President in 2020 – this one a trans-gendered Samoan who is also 1/1024th Navajo and can prove it with her application to law school in Colorado.

Then, I can actually do neither and just sit and read the newest Lee Child or Robert Crais book and pretend Reacher or Joe Pike is a very special friend of mine. Very special.

THE CONTEXT

Since I am compiling the columns into Book 5 (Ammo's Own Pentateuch…) almost a year after they appeared, it is sometimes difficult to remember what was going on even a short twelve months ago.

With the insane 24/7 news cycle, something that appears on a Monday as "the greatest bombshell, walls closing in, beginning of the end for Trump" story can be dead in the water by Thursday and nobody even remembers what the fuss was all about. The "shelf life" of even the most engaging – and possibly, in rare cases, even TRUE -- news story is about three days. Then people either lose interest or the blockbuster story is upstaged by something even worse.

However, the first column in this book appeared on April 6, 2018 and the last one on March 29, 2019. By the last column, President Donald J. Trump, 45th President of the United States, had been in office for 26 full months plus the last eleven days of January, 2017.

With his obvious love of America, the robust economy, secure borders, the beginning of a re-industrialization of the United States and commitment to energy independence, the placid and unified electorate stood solidly behind its non-controversial leader and peace and domestic tranquility were the order of the day. HAHAHAHAHA. I kid. It's what I do.

No. Sadly, almost every day revealed a new stress fracture in the body politic and a new level of mental disorder in the so-called "Resistance". Open the book and you shall see. Travel back with me now and relive just a few of the highlights. Someday, maybe not today, we will all look back and laugh and laugh. And not just because of the Nitrous Oxide.

APRIL, MAY, JUNE, 2018

As always, we begin the New Ammo Grrrll Year in April, which is typically a gorgeous month in Arizona. This quarter begins with an attempt to see a famous meteor shower from a vantage point – Winslow, AZ – put on the map by the Eagles who immortalized it in a lyric in their epic hit, "Take It Easy". Like so many things in life, it did not go as planned.

Shortly thereafter, speaking of "epics", I take off for the umpteenth time on another epic road trip to visit my remaining parent, my 93 year-old Daddy, back in my hometown of Alexandria, Minnesota.

I know you are thinking that a mid-April trip to Minnesota should be smooth sailing weather-wise, but that is because you obviously have never BEEN to Minnesota. It's a sly and crafty little state, weather-wise, and the ONLY month that has never had snowfall is July. Serious spoiler clue.

Moving on, there is a discussion of the importance of a sense of humor to a marriage, and there is another piece about your columnist being mistaken for a short, yet elderly, truck driver.

And near the end of the quarter, just when you think we as a species have hit the highest rung of crazy, we feature a femi-ninny in an elevator who loses what's left of her mind because a man makes a wee joke. Ah, there will BE no joking come the Revolution, Comrades!

Not to be outdone in the Crazy Department, some wretched women who identify as comics though they have never said a humorous thing even by accident, plumb the depths of obscenity by publicly unveiling the dreaded "c-word" in reference to the daughter of the President of the United States.

There then emerges a race to the bottom as to which potty-mouth faux comedienne can call a member of the First Family the most disgusting word.

MAKING LEMONADE

April 6, 2018

You all know the old advice about "When Life gives you lemons, make lemonade." I have never been fond of the saying, to tell you the truth, well-intentioned though it be. For one thing, lemons alone do not make lemonade – you also need a LOT of sugar and fresh, potable water. A lot of "lemony" Life situations – natural disasters, plague, homelessness, war and rationing, to take but a few examples – will find sugar and potable water in short supply.

But I take the point of the saying: in whatever situation you find yourself, however wretched, you can glean a valuable life lesson out of it, turn it to your advantage, or at least have some fun. And so it was for 8 of us in early January.

We had gone to Winslow, Arizona, not just to "stand on the corner" in homage to The Eagles, but to see the Quarantid Meteor Shower, reputed to be well worth the trip. And also to quarter and eat at La Posada Inn, whose Turquoise Room has provided me with several of the best meals I have ever eaten outside of my late, great Mama's dinner table.

We were what at one time would have been considered an interesting and diverse mix of people. Four married couples, ranging in age from 54 to 80. Abby and Ken from Florida; Mr. AG and I from Arizona; Alan and Kaarina, winterers from Palm Springs, residents of Canada, but natives of Britain and Finland; and Ange and John, winterers in Arizona, originally from Indiana and Minnesota.

We were two lawyers, one playwright, homemakers, one retired comic, two engineers, two tech weenies, a yoga instructor; one Scott Johnson groupie (no, really); world travelers who speak six languages among us; pet lovers, Concealed Carriers, insanely proud grandparents, painters, a tap dancer and drumming student; a pianist, composer and band leader; a very good golfer; a woman with a pilot's license, a guy still sporting his full Santa Claus beard from a recent community Christmas parade and his "Elf" wife; Jews, Christians, agnostics, humanists, six conservatives, two socialists, several short women (with Angela the Amazon towering over the rest of us at about 5'6") and several tall men.

If you were keeping score, you realized that was way more than eight people, tribute to the fact that we are all many things at the same time.

But here's the thing, quite remarkable in my opinion: despite these amazing differences and interests, we would have earned not a single point for "diversity," as we were all white, and, to the best of my knowledge, heterosexual and happy with our genders! I suppose the four of us women could have claimed some sort of Diversity Privilege, but that doesn't cut much mustard today. Glory be, we women aren't even allowed to lay claim to being the only people with vaginas! In Lefty Loony Land, there are Tampax dispensers in the Men's Room. Yikes!

Why, some idiot claimed that "Straight black men are the white males of the diversity movement now." Good grief! Haters gotta hate. And losers gotta cling to victimhood like Titanic survivors to a piece of driftwood. As the "tribes" get broken down into ever-smaller units, some category is going to find itself labeled as the Perpetual Bad Guy. Toxic white males as Bad Guys is so yesterday.

Let me ask you this, my friends. If you were at a cocktail party, who would you rather chat up? A beautiful white woman (hint: not me) who can fly a plane, shoot a gun, sell industrial rubber in an all-male industry, and drive a tractor? Or a boring person whose father is half African-American and half Irish and therefore is one quarter "black" and counts as "diverse"?

OMG, Ammo Grrrll said that black people are boring!! No. I absolutely did not. Including my own black and Hispanic foster kids, I know many black people and gay people and Mexican people who are smart, funny, kind, and interesting. What is interesting is not their skin tone or whom they have sex with, but the fact that they can do cool things and are nice people. You know, that wacky old "content of their character" deal MLK appealed to. Why is that so hard to understand?

Well, I'll tell you why. It's because multiple, lucrative industries have grown up around the fact that "Diversity" is all that matters now. And the arbiters of who counts as "Diverse" will decide who counts, thank you very much. And YOU probably don't! Not even Jews and Asians! Discriminated against, yea, systematically murdered, for millenia, Jews are just icky white people who have done too well and ruined the curve and the narrative. Sorry!

So how was the Quarantid Meteor Shower, you ask? Ah, here comes the "lemony" part. A massive cloud cover came in and blocked out the sky entirely for both nights when the Shower was supposed to be showing off.

This did not prevent us from bundling up in all the clothes we had brought to Arizona from Minnesota and going out away from the bright lights of Greater Metropolitan Winslow (pop. 9,754) to lie upon the frozen ground and try to see even one little meteor. It's amazing how invested one can get in thinking one sees it. But it always turned out to be the lights from a plane or a tedious alien spacecraft or some other stupid thing, never the goldarned meteors.

And here comes the "Lemonade" part. After the better part of what felt like many hours, but was probably about 45 minutes, somebody, possibly I, said, "Hey, let's just go drink."

And so, we "made lemonade." We drank lovely exotic martinis, ate beautiful food, laughed and talked and laughed some more, shared experiences, moving and humorous, and got to know each other better. At some point after drinking several pre-drinks before the drinks and wine at dinner, I suggested that we should channel CNN when asked about how awesome the Quarantid Meteor Shower had been, and just bald-faced lie.

"Quarantid Meteor Shower? Oh yeah, it was great."

By the way, the Eagles lyric "standin' on the corner in Winslow, Arizona" has become a cottage industry in itself. There is not only the corner, with Henley and Frey in bronze statues, but now there's a flatbed Ford parked there too for you to photograph. Good times; good times.

COMMON SENSE VEGAN CONTROL

April 13, 2018

Well, let's see. Hitler was a vegetarian; the YouTube shooter was a vegan. Surely, there is an obvious and unfortunate connection between eschewing red meat and wanting to kill people and children. Clearly, we have no choice but to force vegans to register their broccoli, zucchini, arugula, and kale. Especially the kale, which should all be uprooted and the earth around it salted. Vegans may apply for a special permit for these "vile weeds" (per Newman on Seinfeld) to be granted special dispensation if they are served as legal, if unseemly, side dishes placed next to Medium Rare Rib Eyes or Extra Crispy Fried Chicken.

Why any sane person would not prefer shards of hot, crispy potato deep-fried in boiling oil and vigorously over-salted is anyone's guess. But there's no accounting for taste.

It is also well past time to allow Hollywood to make even one more dollar off the promotion of movies that contain weapons. Hollywood celebrity ninnies talk a good game. They make millions from screen violence and then denigrate bitter clingers who have the Audacity to Hope that the right to self-defense also applies to mere mortals. Remember, these are nobodies who have never been mentioned in *People* magazine even once.

The Hollywood Exception ends now with the new Confiscators Go Hogg-Wild Gun Rules.

Any movie that profited from the use of guns must return all the money made off those movies to a Central Bloomberg-Soros Fund to Confiscate All Guns. In the event that this cannot be accomplished either by whining or a boycott of sponsors, a special snowflake posse – The Flaccid Flunkies — shall be recruited to do the confiscating door to door beginning in Texas with the fighting slogan "You go first. No, really, after YOU."

Not only should no movie going forward be allowed to portray the use of a gun, but past movies should be taken to Turner Studios and any reference to or portrayal of a gun should be removed. Hey, if Turner can put color IN, surely they can take weapons OUT. True, *John Wick* will be down to 30 seconds, but that is a small price to pay to avoid the promotion of Things That Go Bang and Murder Our Children. And John Wick's dog will not be killed, but simply sent to a nice farm, since anyone with half a heart would agree that the murder of his dog totally justifies the subsequent 79 deaths by gun, knife, fist and pencil. And that's just a "good start" compared to the carnage in *John Wick 2*. Well, that's my opinion anyway.

Movies should be retitled in a way that promotes peace, light, unicorns, rainbows, and understanding. *Star Wars* will have new life as *Peaceful Coexistence Among the Stars*, and *The Empire Strikes Back* will become *The Empire Hits the Red Reset Button*. Jabba the Hut will not be portrayed as being in any way unattractive just because he is "of size." He will get to know Princess Leia in the Biblical sense. And not just because she's a hostage.

The Longest Day will become *The Shortest Hour*. And *High Noon* will end with Gary Cooper going out for latte and a scone with the bad guys and finding out that it was gender dysphoria and teenage bullying that made them so cranky. It will be retitled *Woke at Noon*.

The provocative Kurt Schlichter has told us repeatedly that "You're gonna hate the new rules." So here is Confiscators Go Hogg-Wild Rule #2: Any politician or Hollywood personage who opens his, her or xer piehole about gun control will not be allowed to have any kind of private bodyguard. And every mansion in Beverly Hills shall have a sign saying, "Not Protected by any kind of Armed Response. Y'all come, hear?" Since every California politician and almost every Hollywood celebrity also pays lip service to support for a Sanctuary State, there will also be a sign with the little silhouetted family holding hands running INTO the house with the word "Bienvenidos" on it. Starting with Nancy Pelosi's mansion, which will be repurposed as a DACA Youth Hostel for MS-13 "kids," no matter how many "teardrop" tats signifying murders they sport.

Finally, the minions and lickspittles behind the Tyrannical Tot Crusade will pass Hogg-Wild Rule #3 — to remove any weapon from X-Box, all electronic devices and video games. The only permitted video game will be Pong. And even then, there will be no mechanism with which to keep score. Keeping score is sexist, racist, and bad for self-esteem. The Default Position of Pong and any future video game will be "Participation Trophy Mode." At the end of every game, a motto shall appear upon the screen saying, "Thanks for playing. You tried really hard. You are not in any way a loser just because you lost."

YOU CAN'T GET HOME AGAIN

April 20, 2018

Thomas Wolfe was quite certain that "You Can't Go Home Again." By which, I took it to mean that we have distorted impressions of people and places seen through the prism of childhood that do not hold up under the harsh light of adulthood. As grownups, we "put away childish things" and move on (unless we are deranged by the 2016 election), and things look different. Plus many things ARE different. Our hometowns themselves change. Dramatically. For example, the old "record store" where we teens hung out, requesting cuts from new albums to be played, is now a tattoo parlor. My father's drugstore is an antique shop.

And yet, we are all destined, yea, obligated, to go home many times in our adult lives. My siblings and I have been blessed to have our parents live well into old age. Mama passed nearly two years ago, but Daddy defies all our expectations and soldiers on. So once again it was my turn to go back home for an extended visit.

I took off at dawn on a splendid 96 degree Monday in April, looking forward to a relaxing trip through the Heartland. New Mexico seems strangely obsessed with convincing drivers that "Dust storms may exist" and posting the guidelines for handling those dust storms with haunting regularity. You would think these rules would be self-evident, but self-evidence seems to be in short supply these days and lawyers roam the land seeking compensation for "victims" who are too stupid to live.

Want me to tell you the guidelines which probably can't be seen in an actual dust storm? Sure, you do. First, do NOT park in the middle of the road or, as they put it, "Do not block the travel lane." Then, "pull over and turn off car." "Do not unbuckle the seat belt" and, finally, "Stay there until it is clear."

Whew! Thank you, New Mexico taxpayers, for all that signage! In the event of a dust storm (which, I now understand, may exist), my plan was to stop short on the dotted white line, leave the engine running, unbuckle my seat belt and open a beer, but you set me straight!

I hit El Paso just past 1:00 p.m. and sailed right on through in record time. One of the reasons that travelers can make such good time in the Southwest is because of our common-sense speed limit of 80 mph. Which, of course, really means 90. Later on, in more populated parts of Texas, the speed limit is lowered to 75 mph, but the drivers continue to go 80-90. It's as if there were a vote and the consensus was "Uh, no. We like that OTHER speed limit better and we intend to go that speed. More or less."

After around 500 miles, I stopped for the night in Van Horn, Texas. I was trying to leave enough time for a good walk, maybe a swim in the hotel pool. And I did leave that time, I just didn't walk or swim, which seemed more trouble somehow than eating and surfing the 'Net. As Miss Scarlett noted, "Tomorrow is another day."

Texas, as you may have heard, is large. So the next day was spent crossing Texas right up to suburban Fort Worth. Again, I had tried to leave room for exercise, and this time I did walk briskly across the street from my hotel to the Chick-Fil-A. And back. Just knowing that New York Mayor de Blasio had tried unsuccessfully to prevent Chick-Fil-A from opening a franchise in Manhattan made that awesome chicken sandwich taste even better.

Wednesday found me in the beautiful Worthington Marriott Renaissance in downtown Fort Worth where I used some of the jillion Marriott points I have accumulated by travel and flagrant credit card abuse. My dear friends, Heather and Bill, joined me for a delightful afternoon and evening. I have achieved Platinum status, which gets you a whole lot of perks, trust me, and all you have to do to get this "free" breakfast buffet is spend 75 nights in a Marriott in one year. Anyone can do it! I think the only level higher is Uranium, except that Hillary sold it all to the Russians somehow without anyone noticing.

And now our travel story gets considerably more harrowing. While strolling about in downtown Fort Worth, which is clean and safe even at night, I was receiving many frantic texts from relatives in Minnesota – plus the Paranoid Texan back home who tirelessly monitors the weather – warning me that a Snow-mageddon style winter storm was headed to Minnesota.

My original plan had been to take a leisurely pace, seeing sights, visiting friends, and, as I may have mentioned, carrying on with my rigorous workout schedule. I was going to arrive in the Twin Cities Saturday, April 14th, with a family dinner set for that evening and a family brunch the next day, leaving for Daddy's Assisted Living place in Alexandria after brunch.

I was invited to stay in Brooklyn Park with my nephew and his lovely wife and have some quality time with Super Baby, their 16-month old son. As the Yiddish expression goes, "Man plans; God laughs." After all the warnings, I was determined to pick up the pace, and arrive ahead of the storm. Which I accomplished by driving exactly 1,000 miles in one of the longest days of my life. In 16 short hours of driving, stopping only for more coffee, gas, and Loves Travel Center's clean restrooms, the temperatures went from 86 in Texas, 84 in Oklahoma, 82 in Kansas, 78 in Missouri, to 68 in Iowa and then plunged to 38 as I crossed into Mordor. A freezing rain had just started up 100 miles from the Twin Cities, complete with a stiff wind. If New Orleans' nickname is The Big Easy, Minnesota should be called The Big Difficulty.

Let me just cut to the chase here. After laying a nice base of ice, the next day the rain turned to snow. And the day after that it continued. Brooklyn Park got sixteen inches of snow. The restaurant where we had scheduled the family get-together was closed at 6:00 p.m., and the staff sent home. Thank God, at least it was a Thai restaurant, so we didn't culturally appropriate. The brunch didn't happen. Even the Minnesota Macho drivers of four-wheel drive vehicles stayed put. I spent not one, not two, but three nights with my gracious nephew and family and not even once did I hear them whisper, "Good Lord, what if she's here till Father's Day!? She keeps muttering that now she doesn't need to feel guilty that she can't get out and walk!"

I didn't get out until Monday, the 16th of flippin' April. But Daddy was very happy to see me. I will be here for twelve days. I heard on the news tonight that another storm system was headed toward Iowa, but it should run its course before I leave. Are there winter storms in May? Anybody along the 35W South corridor or I-10W who would like a houseguest until, say, Mother's Day?

THE HUMOR FACTOR

April 27, 2018

Awhile back on the Ace of Spades blog I read a great quote attributed to Marilyn Monroe: "If you can make a woman laugh, you can make her do anything."

I cannot speak for every woman – though nearly all unelected Grievance Grubbers seem to believe they are qualified to speak for the totality of the aggrieved group he/she/xe represents – but I think there is a lot of truth to what Marilyn said. When you contemplate the glue that holds long-lasting marriages – or, indeed, even friendships – together, the ability to laugh AT (gently) and WITH each other looms large, in my opinion.

I recently lost my longest friendship. My dear friend Carol lost her brave battle with cancer. Carol and I met in second grade. We sat across from one another, started giggling in the manner of 7-year-old little girls, and were friends for the next 65 years. She was my first appreciative "audience"; she laughed at pretty much everything I said, which is a much-prized quality to a future comedienne — though, perhaps, it gives one an unrealistic expectation of how things will go, say, at Union Night in a rough-and-tumble Wisconsin bar.

There is a hole in my world that will never be filled. But this is not meant to be a sad column or even to elicit the sympathy that our kind commenters give us in rocky times. I mean to discuss the importance of humor to a relationship.

As regular readers know, Mr. AG and I have been together for hundreds and hundreds of years. Okay, over half a century. We have very different tastes in food, music, clothes (his are much bigger), books, and art. But we have nearly-identical tastes in movies and comedians. Go know. And we have been making each other laugh for a long, long time.

An old joke about prison acknowledges that men who have spent many years together would soon use up all the jokes they know. A newbie lying in his cell hears someone yell out "62" and everybody laughs like heck. Another guy says "39" with a similar response. The guy asks his cellmate what is going on and he tells him that they have numbered their stock of jokes to save time. The newbie wants in on the fun and yells "44". Nobody laughs. He asks his cellmate why nobody laughed and he says, "Timing."

Families and long-married couples will also develop a kind of shorthand to remind them of shared experiences. Let me give you two examples.

The first example is from my "family of origin," as it is called in therapy. My mother did not countenance swearing, but even more than vulgarity she hated when we kids were mean to each other. She particularly hated us telling each other to "shut up." Once when I was about 10 and my sister about 5 Daddy was driving us uptown and a man stepped out from between two parked cars. Daddy slammed on the brakes to avoid hitting him. Daddy said a naughty word and my sister chimed in with the worst word she knew: "Daddy, that is just a shut-up man." Forever after, when someone might deserve a description as a Son Of a $#%^&, we would say, "Now, there is a real shut-up man." Okay, it's not hilarious to anyone else; it is a private in-joke – every healthy family has them — but it amused us for decades.

The second example is from our son when he was also about 5. One evening he was pretending to be a detective. He had a small notebook and was interrogating his grandma, his father, and me and making notes on our responses to questions about a pretend crime. By his grandma's name he had written an "R"; by mine, an "LW" and by his father's, a "VW." When asked what his abbreviations meant, he said, "I felt that Grandma was acting Regular; Mom was acting a Little Weird and Daddy was acting Very Weird." And so was born a secret code for categorizing people we meet as Regular, a Little Weird, and Very Weird. You can nudge your spouse and whisper "LW" and no one is the wiser. Feel free to use it.

By the way, the older I get, the more convinced I become that there ARE no "Regulars." Virtually every one of us is a Little Weird. And that's OK.

When I shared Marilyn's quote that "if you can make a woman laugh, you can make her do anything," Mr. AG brightened. "Can you make her cook and clean?" Evidently.

I remember reading (another) great column by Dave Barry wherein he questioned the evidence that women prize a "sense of humor" as they are constantly asserting on dating sites. I am paraphrasing from memory now, but he wondered aloud where all these alleged humor-loving females were when he was in high school because it seemed to him that what they prized then was "hotness" in the form of athletic ability or a cool car. He had wit up the wazoo and yet apparently was not considered a good catch back then. (He has done very well since.)

I am very blessed with funny friends besides my best friend, Mr. AG. My walking partner, The Paranoid Texan, could have been a standup. There's Barb and her two hilarious sons, Bonnie, Heather, Angela — all are people who can make me shriek with laughter to the distress of passersby or other restaurant patrons. And, of course, our immense stock of witty commenters routinely cracks me up.

Highbrow wit is all well and good and Mr. AG can be very droll and witty. But do not discount just plain silliness as a day-maker. The other day Mr. AG insinuated that I did not know how to "gallop" properly or shoot with my finger the way kids played cowboy in the halcyon days of the '50s when biting your bologna into the shape of a gun and going "bang" at your cafeteria-mate would not get you indefinitely suspended from school.

Mr. AG's completely unfounded and almost-certainly sexist accusation quickly resulted in a challenge and mad galloping around the house, slapping our thighs and making horse sounds, hiding around corners and aiming with our fingers. A stranger coming upon the sight would have called some sort of Agency charged with carting off the senile and denying us the right to own weapons. But we had a lot of fun in the brief time before I pulled a thigh muscle. I certainly don't remember that being a problem galloping around the "'hood." Memo to self: galloping now out; maybe a slow trot, or calm canter, so as not to irritate my "shut-up" thigh.

SAFE AT HOME

May 4, 2018

Wonderful are the words "SAFE AT HOME," whether in baseball or in life. The doctor I see for my annual checkup every five or six years always asks me if I "feel safe at home," and I always assure him that I do. Then he asks whether there are firearms in the home. And I say, "Yes. That's why I feel safe."

Other lovely words are "Love," "Peace," "It's Benign," "Not Guilty," and "Hillary will never be President!"

I had intended to take a leisurely five-and-a-half days, driving just 400 miles a day, to do the 2200 miles home, but in the end the "horse smelled the barn" and the car just kept going. On the second day of the journey home, I drove from Guthrie, OK all the way to Las Cruces, NM, just over 700 miles. The last 370 miles from Cruces to my front door felt like a trip to the grocery store.

Even though I had had an oil change and new filters while in Minnesota, my mileage home was not spectacular. The headwinds all the way were fierce. Those Dust Storm Alarmists I wrote about two weeks ago turned out to be not just whistlin' Dixie. (If, indeed, it is even still legal to whistle Dixie. Or to use a Dixie cup. Or to listen to the Dixie Chicks. It's only a matter of time...)

On a trip like this, I must maintain eternal vigilance for all the things the Road Sign People have taken the time to warn me about: falling rock, the aforementioned dust storms, ice on bridges, accidentally killing highway workers and incurring that darned $10,000 fine, and hitchhiking escapees from prison. It's a lot to keep in mind.

Mr. AG knows in his heart that one day I will have the following conversation with a hitchhiker:

Me: Where you headed?
HHiker: Oh, nowhere special. Just out of here.
Me: You aren't by any chance an escaped prisoner?
HHiker: Ha, ha, certainly not! I just like orange jumpsuits.
Me: That's what I figured. Hop in. Could you hold my purse and gun while I put in this CD? Safety first, right?

In truth, any self-respecting hitchhiker would hurl himself from the car the fourth time through on "repeat" of the soundtrack from *Man of La Mancha*.

I am also ever alert for what I call Nuggets of Joy. They aren't hard to find. This is such a spectacularly beautiful country. Leaving Guthrie, OK on a peaceful Sunday at 6 am, with a yuge full moon still hanging low in the sky, and a developing fuchsia sunrise in my rearview, I couldn't help but say a little prayer of thanks. I had the road mostly to myself until well after noon and finally figured out why. Everybody in Oklahoma and Texas was in church.

There is also plenty of Fodder for Fun. On Hwy 44 West, I passed a liquor store that offered to "cash your paycheck here." What a service – loved by wives everywhere! What could possibly go wrong? A few miles down the road from that, I noticed a sign for The Feedlot Restaurant. Surely, customers in cattle country must be aware that the sole purpose of a "feedlot" is to fatten the cattle for market? Is this an attractive inducement for a restaurant?

Not long after there were signs ordering drivers to "Pull over for poultry inspection." I did not think they meant me, but after 3 weeks in a car that made the Joads' vehicle look tidy, it seemed possible that it could contain a live chicken.

I stopped for a meal in that gray area between breakfast and lunch when thrifty restaurant owners typically send most of their wait staff home. I was the only person in the little cafe, save for one earnest young waiter who felt I would like to chat.

The first thing he asked me was "Are you a truck driver?" Now I took no offense for several reasons. First, truck driving is a noble profession and I have seen some women drivers, though usually in couples and not alone. Secondly, it is kind of like being asked if you are pregnant. True, it probably means you are chubby, but it is also flattering in late, late middle age to be thought CAPABLE of getting pregnant. So, it's a toss-up.

In this instance I was wearing my second-best boots, new bluejeans, and a pro-Second Amendment t-shirt under a plaid shirt from Dillards' Reba collection. I would not be mistaken for Donna Reed, in her ever-present heels and pearls, but I thought I looked plenty spiffy. What would make the little dear think that a five foot tall woman on the wrong side of 70 was a truck-driver, I could not guess. But I determined to up my game and possibly wear makeup and a dress for the rest of the journey.

The experience also made me think about applying for a part-time job driving truck, since I am a Driving Machine and evidently already own the outfit.

Here would be my application: elderly woman seeks part-time employment for short or long hauls. She has no CDL license, but if pulled over will declare the truck to be a "Sanctuary Truck" not subject to the laws applicable to The Little People. Speaking of little, she is not only old, but short, and will need some sort of ladder or hoist and derrick to get into the truck. She does get lost at least once virtually every day of a trip, even with an exasperated Garmin. But, on the plus side, hits road workers only infrequently, and always carries $10,000 in cash just in case. In the event of engine trouble, or a flat, she will have no choice but to sit crying beside the road until some welcome toxic male comes along. She will need every Tuesday off for her regular poker game.

When you see a semi whizzing down the road with no obvious driver visible over the windshield, double clutchin' and playing with the horn obnoxiously, that might be me. Feel free to wave.

HOMECOMING LAWSUIT

May 11, 2018

In these dark and terrifying days of a Literal Hitler in the Oval Office (who wears a yarmulke when he visits the Western Wall in Jerusalem, the eternal capital of the Jewish people and soon to be the home of the DJT American Embassy, Hotel, and Casino), one has to take inspiration where one can find it.

And I have been greatly inspired by the Democrat Party's Losing Loser Lawsuit, filed in a loser-ly fashion more than a year after the 2016 election. Which Hillary lost.

It may shock regular readers to learn that I was not elected as Homecoming Queen in my senior year of high school. Spurred on by the courageous if clinically insane example of the Perez/Ellison DNC Lawsuit, I am suing every member of my class. Also included are the School Board (most of whose members are now technically, deceased), and – but, of course! — the Russians, who I hope don't actually show up in court like they did with Moronic Mueller's Magical, Mystical Inquisition, Indictment and Fishing Trip. (Could anything be funnier on this earth? Except the PROSECUTION asserting that the Russkies weren't served properly and should go home for three weeks while they, their Inquisitors, get it right? Oh Lord, parody is dead…but we must try to carry on.)

The year in which my tragic miscarriage of electoral justice occurred would be 1964. Ah, I hear you say, isn't that, uh, kind of a LONG time ago? Shouldn't you maybe be over it by now? Nonsense! Why, just the other day I read on the Internet that a woman has come forward to say that Tom Brokaw kissed her once on a couch fifty years ago. FIFTY

YEARS AGO. Yay! She gets to be a member of the #MeToo Club.

Speaking of unspeakable assault, I am filing an additional posthumous lawsuit against Eustis Q. Bloominfarter, (not his real name, and also dead), for snapping my bra in the hallway in 7th grade. This was a common thing that adolescent idiot boys (but I repeat myself) used to do to us few young ladies who had reached puberty earlier than some of our other classmates. Decades of therapy have helped me get over the trauma. Of having to beat the crap out of him. Seventh grade was the last year before The Great Testosterone Advantage kicked in when it was still possible for a righteous 75-lb. girl to beat up an annoying boy.

My lawsuit for the Stolen Homecoming Election may not be as persuasive as the Democrat Party's Loser Lawsuit. I mean, at least Hillary was on the ballot.

Which I was not.

But without the Russian interference, I'm sure there could have been a vigorous write-in campaign for me. I am also suing the Episcopal Church for transferring the minister father of my two best friends from Alexandria to Edina right before our senior year. With those two votes, and the massive influence as Thought Leaders that the twins wielded, the whole outcome might have been different.

Had Hillary not been a Losing Loser, the "fundamental transformation" of America would have been well into its tenth year instead of dead in the water. Known primarily for her zany madcap pratfalls, Hillary would have put the "fun" back in "fundamental" transformation! Open borders, Australian-style gun grabbing, taxes raised, coal killed, oil production outsourced, Louis Farrakhan as UN Ambassador,

Loretta "Tarmac" Lynch as Chief Justice of the Supreme Court, regulations increased, Oh, my! The differences would have been yuge. But what about the differences in MY life, hmmm?

Instead of being a happily married wife and mother and retired comedienne, living in a modest but very comfortable house in a Dusty Little Village with wonderful friends and neighbors, I could have been all that AND a former Homecoming Queen. Maybe I would have even got to keep the tiara. That's how different my life would have been!

So, you can see why I would want a second bite at that apple. Let's review the facts:

There were three young ladies on the Homecoming Queen ballot, each of them plenty cute, Boy Howdy! One of the sweetest, nicest, smartest girls, named Carole, won. She was also really pretty then and, sad to report, has changed very little since. I'm hoping we can have lunch before or after her deposition, if she doesn't take it too personally.

In 1964, Nikita Krushchev, five foot-three inch snappy dresser and Weight-Watcher drop-out, was the recently deposed Head Honcho of the Soviet Union. He had given a peculiar speech to the Comintern in which he asserted that "half of my opponent's supporters are nothing but a Basket of Rotten Turnips who support Stalinism, Imperialism, Capitalism, and the Right to Rent a Studio Apartment with Fewer than 15 People In It."

While the average Russian citizen wondered aloud where to find the line for the rotten turnips, their Communist Commisar overlords nudged Krushchev into retirement with the gentle promise: "We LIKE Stalinism, fattie! Go quietly and we probably won't kill you."

Speculation abounded that Nikita had become unhinged from being bitterly disappointed when his much anticipated trip to Disneyland during his state visit in 1959 had to be canceled for security reasons. Looking for a way to exact revenge, he obviously selected a random teenage American Grrrll, plotted for five years, and then purchased $12.95 worth of Facebook ads, no wait, there WAS no Facebook yet — just faces and books. No, what I meant to say, he put ads in the mighty and influential local paper, The Park Region Echo, and threw his considerable bulk behind making sure I got no votes for Queen. Not one, not even my own.

I'm pretty sure that was how it happened. Either that, or I failed to visit Wisconsin.

A LUNATIC IN THE LIFT

May 18, 2018

By now, as frequently happens with a weekly column, this is pretty old news. But it's in my wheelhouse, so I thought I would weigh in. Besides, I'm still mad. Regular readers may think they have seen me mad before, but that was just warm-up. The Safe Space Dwellers want to talk about "triggers"? Consider me triggered. As my hero Mark Steyn says, "Stand well back!"

Straw – meet camel's back. For far too long, we have caved like cheap card tables in the war against the Productive by the Pretend Oppressed, often for good reasons. We have been threatened with lawsuits, boycotts, loss of employment, and subjected to vicious ginned-up Twitter and Facebook attacks. First, the Professionally Offended always demand some kind of groveling apology. As I hope Kanye has learned, NEVER EVER APOLOGIZE. First, you have done nothing wrong. Second, it doesn't ever work.

Groveling apologies have the same effect on left-wing bullies as liquor did revving up lynch mobs.

We need a new name for Social Justice Warriors, for sure. There is not one thing "just" about shouting down speakers, running around with masks breaking windows, or driving cake bakers out of business. The psycho ninnies attracted to such actions are also not very "social." And they are the opposite of "warriors." They are generally cowards and babies.

And so here are the facts: a gentleman named Richard Ned Lebow of King's College, London was in a crowded elevator ("Lift" in Brit talk) at the San Francisco Hilton at an academic conference a couple of months ago. As buttons were being pushed for floors, from the back of the elevator, Mr. Lebow joked, "Ladies' lingerie, please." And a woman named Simona Sharoni said nothing in the elevator, but freaked out when she returned to her coven. And she did what any miserable, rage-aholic looking for attention would do under the circumstances – she consulted the Manual of Unauthorized Behavior and then fired off a letter to the association's director, claiming to be "shaken," though apparently not stirred.

Mr. Lebow certainly didn't touch her, God forbid. He didn't ask her to watch him shower. He didn't carry a replica of her bloody severed head, which we were assured by our betters was a laugh riot. He didn't ask a buddy to snap a photo of him pretending to grab her breasts. Nobody in the elevator was advised to "put some ice on that." All he did was make a mild, completely harmless little joke to break the usual tension that almost everyone who isn't insane experiences in a crowded elevator.

In the long forgotten Victorian Era, one had to refer to a chair or piano "leg" as a "limb." The word "leg" was so triggering to Victorian ladies that they would have to lie down on a fainting couch. Today's "strong," "independent" feminists have brought us full circle to where hearing "ladies' lingerie" is an occasion for virtual fainting. And then A Grievously and Perpetually Offended Woman has to run right off and tattle to Big Daddy Executive Director. That's one tough cookie of a feminist! In the event of trouble, I want nobody on my team who is rendered limp and "shaken" by the words "ladies' lingerie." Or by any mere words.

This great feminist hero, possibly angling for a job on MSNBC, declared AFTER the first round of apologies by Mr. Lebow – which, of course, were inadequate and unacceptable — "I have dedicated my life to confronting sexism and I cannot and will not remain silent when misogyny is in play." To which I, a not insane woman, would say: "Bite me."

I would add: you are a humorless, wretched, petty, vindictive twit, looking for an occasion for self-aggrandizement and a "leg up" in whatever airless space you occupy. You are nothing more than an adult-like version of the same prissy little grade school tattletales who told Teacher of petty infractions that occurred while she was out of the room. Your ilk were the reason I spent a lot of time clapping erasers and sitting in the hall. You were always girls – why was that? Boys could be many annoying things, but they were rarely tattletales.

Ms. Sharoni: You get a lot of money to teach not one, but two, frivolous, unserious subjects that make my Sociology major look positively dignified – Women's and now "Gender" Studies. My advice would be to go quietly about peddling your unscholarly, indoctrinating crap under the radar in the hopes that nobody really notices how useless you are and continues to give you a paycheck. But where's the fun in that when you can torture a "white man" who mentions "ladies' lingerie" in an elevator? There's a better than even chance that you can take away his livelihood by pretending in the most disgustingly dishonest way that you were harmed somehow. And wouldn't THAT be a feather in your tinfoil hat?!

Where were the other women in this tempest in a thimble? Did not even one defend Mr. Lebow? If not, you cowardly, bleating sheeple, we have nothing in common but lady bits.

For example, I am generally a happy person, looking for ways to amuse or uplift others. I enjoy every single part of my day, starting with my morning walk with the Paranoid Texan who makes many, many jokes, not one of which do I parse for "sexism" or "misogyny." I laugh and see if I can top his joke or "riff" on it. Men who enjoy my company, without exception, LIKE women. Later, Mr. AG comes out of his man cave for a little brunch and we eat and joke together although, sometimes, I must confess, he does touch me. Oh, icky poo. Boy cooties! No, wait…I remember now: I LIKE both joking AND being touched. Because I am not insane.

Then I go into my office and write for a bit and surf the Net, hoping to stay upbeat and not read about people like Ms. Sharoni. I might read a mystery or go to the Tactical Range, or do some laundry or call my elderly Papa. Later, I might go out to a local diner with Mr. AG. If we find ourselves in an elevator, we always arrive at our floor without a nervous breakdown. Because we are not insane. In the evening, we might watch a Jason Statham action movie or an old sitcom episode or have a few friends in for drinks or go watch the Diamondbacks win. Then we read and snuggle in bed and rest up for the next day which we expect to enjoy just as much as the one we just spent. If it's Tuesday, there's poker!

See how that works? Happy! Just live and let live. As the Psalmist advises: "This is the day the Lord hath made. Let us rejoice and be GLAD in it." The Psalmist said that because finding occasion to be glad, rather than professionally and perpetually offended, makes even a difficult life bearable. Also, he was not insane.

PROMISES, PROMISES

May 25, 2018

Regular readers know that I recently made a long road trip. But, it really doesn't matter if I'm only driving two miles to the Walmart — basically, I cannot drive without music.

My eclectic driving soundtracks range from Brahms' Second Piano Concerto to Broadway show tunes to Toby Keith's sensitive love ballad, "Get Out of Your Clothes or Get Out of My Car." (Our son once told us that "if you want to clear the room of chicks" that the band Rush will do the trick. Similarly, if I want Mr. AG to leave the house, all I have to do is play Toby Keith's Red Solo Cup. In fact, the mere THREAT to play it can shape him right up.)

My compilation CDs for travel are not universally appreciated. Obviously, tastes differ. But I am guessing that there would be wide agreement that the Eagles would be considered quintessential road music. I typically began each driving day on my recent journey with their Greatest Hits ("The Very Best of") CD. That – and the third cup of coffee – woke me up enough to prepare me for the first 2-300 miles. I love the tight harmonies, the familiar, warble-along lyrics, the "greater than the sum of the parts" effect of the musicians.

I am particularly fond of bassist Timothy B. Schmit, whose sweet voice stars in just a couple of tunes, my favorite of which is "Love Will Keep Us Alive." However, as with many, many pop songs, it does not behoove one to think too deeply about the lyrics, starting with the debatable premise in the title. Unfortunately, I had a LOT of time on my hands in my recent 5,000-mile trip, and I behooved up a storm. Yes, it is true that love is very important to keeping one alive, but the occasional sammich and a glass of water do help.

In confessing the extent of their love, the 3 songwriters (Pete Vale, Jim Capaldi and Paul Carrack) and Mr. Schmit make several extravagant promises. Not least of which is "I would die for you," and "I would climb the highest mountain." Men are always promising things of this nature in song. They swear they will swim the deepest ocean, lasso the stars and the moon, or climb a mountain – and not just any old high hill, always the "highest," like a hyperbolic President Trump speech, bless his little heart!

Now, first of all, I do not know a single woman who has ever requested such physical tests of devotion because, among many problems, they would involve long ABSENCES. What is to become of her while you are off dog-paddling across the Pacific? Who will kill the spiders and reach high shelves while you trudge up Everest? Then there is the issue of how many men can remotely accomplish such feats. Mr. AG, for example, swims like an anvil. I would not want him in the deep end of the pool, much less tackling the deepest sea.

When we examine these promises, however heartfelt they sound, what is the common denominator in all of them? Nobody – not even Michael Phelps or Bruce "Caitlyn" Jenner – can deliver on them! Now I am not suggesting for even a moment that they are just insincere and cunning ways to get you into bed. I am simply saying that as promises go, these particular ones are guaranteed to be as meaningless as "If you like your doctor, you can keep your doctor."

And I am here, as a service to male love song writers everywhere to suggest more realistic promises to indicate undying love for your woman. The great Brad Paisley has already covered putting the toilet seat down. Here are just a few more ideas. Read and learn, fellas.

I will clean your Kimber 1911 with its 47 parts
And its special tiny takedown tool and springs that fly like darts.

I will do the taxes you detest, to rid you of your tension,
I already guessed you'd start too late, and filed for an
extension.

I will ask if you are losing weight; though the opposite is
clear.
And just to show I mean it, say: "Here's a cupcake, dear!"

I will let you use the bathroom first when we get to a hotel.
No need to go in detail why, but to say it's just as well.

See how USEFUL and CONCRETE these promises are? With verifiable results, just like Obama's Late, Great Iran Nuclear Deal…oh wait…that was more in the vein of swimming the deepest ocean. Or rather sending a very deep ocean of hard cold cash to Ms. Jarrett's homies in Iran on the hilarious pretext that maybe, possibly, later, the pathological lying mullahs won't go nuclear. Unless they feel like it. What could go wrong with taking the word of a "Death to America" culture that states that deliberate lying to infidels is not only allowed, but recommended?

But I digress. Women never sing songs promising proof of their love through triathlon-style physical challenges. And here – despite all the gender nonsense – we see a very basic difference between males and females. A love song aimed at men, promising the sun, the moon, the stars, will be an epic failure with its target audience. Men will say, "Hey, the sun, the moon, all that crap, love 'em, babe. Oceans are cool, especially in the Sports Illustrated Swimsuit issue. But you know what would be really great? If you got naked!"

If we are honest here, isn't getting the woman into bed either the explicit theme or the subtext of virtually every love song in existence? (See: "Let's Get It On," "Lay, Lady Lay," "Let It Snow," "Baby Ima Want You," "I Can't Get No Satisfaction," "Lay Down Sally," ad infinitum…)

The underlying theme of almost every pop song from a woman to a man is, "Why yes, I WILL have sex with you." In real life, we may couch that promise in what we believe is more romantic terms, "Honey, tonight why don't I make you a homemade meatloaf sandwich on your favorite bread, and we'll watch some sports on TV, and then we'll go to bed early?"

And the man will take notice and say, "What a great idea! Except how about we have the sex NOW and then maybe watch sports and eat? I mean, the game might be really good and we could get distracted and accidentally forget about the sex."

It's not easy to capture that kind of commitment to romance in a song.

OH, THE FUN WE'LL HAVE WHEN WE ACT LIKE THEM!

June 1, 2018

As the brilliant and funny Kurt Schlichter says repeatedly: "You guys are gonna hate the new rules." And we have so many of those new rules now; it's time to redeem a few of those "Get Out of Acting Like a Civilized Grownup Free" Cards.

Let's start with emulating Obama's buddies in Iran and open every morning bell of the Stock Exchange and every session of Congress by chanting "Death to the Country du Jour!" One day it could be Iran; the next day, Cuba, or Yemen; the day after that, Germany. (Ally, schmally; I hold grudges.) Remember, they started it.

Think of the opportunity it would afford for entrepreneurs to manufacture different flammable flags. Naturally, the flag of the Country of the Day would be set ablaze. Instead of The Great Satan and the Little Satan – such cleverness can scarcely be topped – we will call the designated Death-To country The Big Doody-Head. And its smaller ally "The Little Poop in the Pants." A subsidiary business to the flammable flag industry would be making dummy likenesses of each country's leader. These could be burned like the flag, or merely hanged.

In 2008, some madcap gay boys in California hanged a likeness of Sarah Palin on their front porch until their less unhinged neighbors persuaded them to take it down. Countless people have made likenesses of President Trump as targets of abuse. Not just current officeholders could be available "effigy-ready"; even has-beens like Hillary and non-celebrities like your neighbor who starts leaf-blowing at

7:01 am (HOA compliant by a full minute) could be special ordered with an enclosed photo.

A third marketing opportunity would be for bloody severed heads of such notables as Shower Boy Weinstein, Teen Texter Weiner, Girlfriend Beater Schneiderman, sports figures in bad slumps, teachers you didn't like, whoever. We can all just wander around with our own personal severed head. Something that classy should not be confined to just one nasty, foul-mouthed, brain-dead anorexic. Only Deplorable wet blankets failed to find the humor in posing with a bloody severed head of the President of the United States. A chicken in every pot and a bloody severed head for every merry prankster!

But wait...there's more! Moving right along, we now realize that throwing beverages at restaurant patrons with different opinions from our own, is like, totally righteous and also quite humorous. It is especially good fun if that person is with her mother. Haha. Good to know.

This should make dining out quite the adventure going forward when the ante is upped from water to red wine to hot coffee. It's all good. Haters deserve it. Guess that tired old "War on Women" theme is so yesterday. Read the comments in the various leftist publications chortling over the assault on Tomi Lahgren. Heck, it was a laugh riot. We will expect the same reaction when we do it. Goose, meet Gander. Find out where Anderson Cooper or Rachel Maddow or Al Sharpton has brunch and bring a garden hose. There's no such thing now as a moisture-free lunch or a peaceful brunch. That option is off the table.

Remember, they started it.

There was near-universal leftist hand-wringing over the Hamas body count (some of which bodies were surprisingly lively in their shrouds, perhaps in premature anticipation of their sweaty 72-virgin screw-a-thon). All those poor Palestinians had done to the awful Jooz was light hundreds of tires on fire, and have squads of known terrorists ready to go on a murderous rampage if the women and children breached the wall. Oh, they also sent incendiary kites over the wall. You know, a typical peaceful protest. And the Jooz had the temerity to take no casualties.

I have already begun to stockpile old tires and kites in anticipation of obtaining one of those Hollywood Maps of the Stars' Gated Mansions. Remember, celebs: no shooting! You hate both guns AND border walls, so get ready to learn the words to "Joshua Fit the Battle of Jericho" cuz your walls are definitely going to "come tumblin' down."

Finally, there will be mass kneeling. No, not kneeling at Mass, that's a given. We will kneel everywhere – in the aisles of Walmart to protest the injustice of not stocking plain Corn Doritos; during high school fight songs to protest some athletes having a disparity of talent; in the main entrance to the Dorothy Chandler Pavilion to protest the absence of Jason Statham or Dwayne Johnson in the Hottest, Manliest Actor Category. We will kneel on the beaches, we will kneel in the workplace, we will kneel in the Post Office line to make the line go even slower. All kneeling, all the time! Except for Tim Tebow. Kneeling to pray not allowed!

For protesters too lazy even to kneel, you can always stage a die-in at your local supermarket. Protest doesn't get any easier than this. Lying down pretending to be dead in hopes of disarming law-abiding Americans while simultaneously inconveniencing shoppers is – evidently – totally legal! However, nudging the "corpses" lightly with your steel-toed boots to determine whether they are as dead as advertised is not legal. Bear that in mind, no matter how tempting it might be. Accidentally dropping a dozen eggs, or spilling a full 2-lb pail of Karo Syrup on the hair of some of the corpses would fall into that grey area of legality. It might be better to check with your attorney in advance of a clumsy accident. Remember, you can channel Clapper and say you were trying to "help." I'm pretty sure the Jets owner said he will pay any fines you incur.

Order your Full Leftist Fun Kit now while supplies last – a unisex severed head with multiple Mr. Potato Head-style accessories and wigs, a flammable flag, a limp starter dummy of Hillary including a variety of ugly yet pricey 2XL pantsuits in heavy quilted burlap for summer; a full set of used radials, several kites, some Antifa masks, and Presidential Kneepads! Act before midnight to receive a large water glass in a generic enough design to blend into the stemware of any restaurant. Karo Syrup not included. (Karo is the dreaded High-Fructose Corn Syrup and cannot be handled safely. It is thick, viscous, supernaturally sticky, and would take forever to wash out of hair. Word.)

Please note: Dummy Hillary doll Not Available in Wisconsin.

SMARMY DANIELS

June 8, 2018

I am probably almost alone in the fact that I have never watched Smarmy Daniels and the lawyer who looks like a sleazebag someone ordered from Central Casting: "Hymie, get me a guy who looks like a shyster!" I do not watch CNN – ever, because I also do not fly – so I have only seen Smarmy and her mouthpiece in a few brief glimpses on the Internet and have never even heard her voice. I am not interested in the story; I am not obsessed with other people's love lives, because I have one of my own.

I also do not care if President Trump – then just regular old Donald Trump – either had sex with Smarmy, or paid her alleged "hush money." It could not have been hush money because she hasn't hushed. You know what I have even less respect for than a blabbermouth extortionist porn star? A blabbermouth extortionist porn star WHO WON'T STAY BOUGHT!

Man, if someone gave me $130,000 to keep quiet — about sex or pretty much anything — my lips would be sealed. Go ahead, try me! In business, in my personal life, my WORD is my bond, never mind a legal contract! I guess that is old-fashioned if there's more money to be made from blabbing. I read that she was getting $75,000 a NIGHT to take off her clothes. You can search the Archives of my column for a single anti-male word, but, good heavens, fellas, you guys can be idiots! What kind of cover charge could that entail? Why on earth would a man pay that to see lady bits he can see any night on regular old cable television?

And just parenthetically, there is no such thing as a "former" porn star. Unless the technology changes drastically, those

DVD's or tapes or YouTubes are forever, honey. Ask Paris Hilton.

We "alt-right" Bitter Bible-Clinging, gun-totin' Lady Deplorables are supposed to really care about this. I don't. And here's why: I LOVE Donald Trump! There, I've said it. Every Democrat campaign ad I ever saw in Minnesota ends with: "Vote for Quisling H. Commsymp! The Democrat who fights for YOU!" Well, Donald J. Trump fights for ME. And America. Nobody has for a long time. Even more important, he is committed to allowing me to keep more of my own money and my own weapons to fight for MYSELF.

"But, but, but…how COULD you love Trump? You're a WOMYN! He's so crude, so unfaithful to his many wives; twelve years ago, he used the word 'pussy' in a jokey conversation he stupidly thought was private!"

Yes, I know all that. And still do not care. Hugely; I hugely do not care. I would not choose him for a husband, not even with his many billions. And I'm sure he would be crushed to know that. Not a one of his many wives has been short, average looking on her best day, or his age. All of which I am. So I guess he will just have to make do with the tall, beautiful Melania. But, see, I was voting for a President, not a husband, get the difference?

Oh Lord, it's great to see a real street fighter on our side for a change! The three major networks, MSNBC, CNN, the New York Times, the Washington Post and the tedious Never Trumpers seem to get their talking points memo from the DNC every morning. To wit: "Today: Stormy; Trump said all immigrants are animals; Israel disproportionate; Trump is a Nazi, and more Stormy. If you lose this, yesterday's memo was identical. Consider it the Default Memo going forward. Thank you." Then they launch into full spittle-flecked attack mode. I am GLAD when the President fights back. It made me despairing and demoralized when W (whom I also liked very much) refused to defend himself, and by extension, his base.

Once Trump got the nomination and the field was narrowed to a mendacious, humorless, greedy, influence peddler with a penchant for wiping computers, like, with a cloth, or an orange-haired reality star who was against open borders, for the First and Second Amendments, and a strong supporter of Israel, there was no contest. Not one second of dithering. November 9, 2016 was one of the five or six happiest days of my life. Made ten times as sweet by all the caterwauling bawl-baby leftists losing what was left of their minds.

Not only has President Trump not disappointed me — with all he has accomplished DESPITE the Obama-appointed court jesters and many spineless, maneuvering Republican backstabbers, plus a 98% hostile media, academy, entertainment complex, and several billionaire oligarchs funding mayhem — he has succeeded beyond my wildest dreams. And is still getting wind in his sails!

The sleeping giant of Deplorables is usually too busy supporting the layabouts and raising the next generation of taxpayers and military personnel to devote much attention to politics. But now we sense one last chance to stem the tsunami of political correctness and cultural rot. Heck, there's even a slim chance with McCain (may he not die, but recover and retire in gratitude) and Flake gone, those Senate seats could flip to Republican!

Forward the march to save our Constitutional Republic and Make America Great Again.

Trump/Pence 2020; Pence/Haley 2024; Pence/Haley 2028; Haley/Candace Owens/2032! Who knows what surprising conservative could arise after that? But by the next couple of election cycles after President Haley, I will likely shuffle off this mortal coil and finally be eligible to vote Democrat – at least twice.

Oh, I also wouldn't be averse to some kind of "job-sharing" gig for Diamond and Silk as Presidential Press Secretaries in one of those early administrations. Picture Jim Acosta double-teamed by those two forces of nature!

I am agog at the patience, brains, and fighting spirit of Sarah Huckabee Sanders. Whatever she's being paid, it should include combat pay. I'm pretty sure I would have gone full John Wick by the third Press Conference. "Asked and answered ten times, you speechifying, blathering, biased, bigoted, boring, brain-dead bimbo grandstander," is probably not an approved response in the Press Secretary's Manual — even to a woman. Let alone aimed at what passes for men in that funhouse reality world where genders outnumber brain cells.

THE THIRD RAIL

June 15, 2018

For decades now, we have heard that the "third rail" in politics – untouchable without inviting electrocution – was the Social Security System.

And now a different sort of Third Rail has been grabbed. The lovely daughter of the President of the United States, communing with her beautiful baby, no less, is called a "feckless c*nt" by another woman. Charming. Long ago, in a galaxy far far away, I used to own a copy of a feminist bible called *Sisterhood is Powerful*. Right. Some Sisterhood!

Ah, how far we have come from the civilized days when Democrat President Truman wrote a letter to a critic who panned his daughter's musical talent in which he said, "Some day I hope to meet you. When that happens you'll need a new nose, a lot of beefsteak for black eyes and perhaps a supporter below!"

Or earlier yet, when Democrat Andrew Jackson challenged a duelist because Jackson's enemies had put the man up to an insinuation of indecency directed at Jackson's beloved wife, Rachel. His enemies knew that Jackson's code of honor would not allow him to let it slide. The man they picked to deliver the insult was a crack shot duelist. They figured it would be a good way to get rid of Old Hickory. Jackson let him fire first; took the large round to the shoulder, and then killed the man dead.

My experience as a person who identifies as a woman on account of that's what I am has been that the "third rail" of unacceptable naughty words for almost all women is the "c-word."

And so the race to the bottom for unfunny, potty-mouthed "comediennes" has been temporarily "won" by Samantha Wasp. Mosquito. Scorpion. Some annoying, stinging insect or other, possibly a Gnat. However, as Mr. AG says several times a day, there IS no bottom. So it will somehow be surpassed, probably within a week or two.

We've had bloody severed heads, threats to kill public figures (haha, just kidding, they always say when called out), weepy fake apologies, angry retractions of the fake apologies, middle finger salutes, endless "effenheimers," the excruciating public attack on Sarah Huckabee Sanders at a dinner for miserable tools with dead brains and deader souls.

Among these wretched, self-defined "nasty women" of the Left, who posture as tough by their foul mouths, not one had the cojones to disagree with calling a mother a c*nt. Quite the opposite, in fact. A couple of mediocre actresses – Minnie Driver? Sally "You like me! You really like me!" Field – not only supported Ms.Gnat, but said that "c*nt" was not an accurate description because Ivanka was not "deep" enough to be called that. Oh, to be that witty!

And a couple of man-like substances weighed in. And I do mean weighed in. Michael "Tub O'Goo" Moore put down his Krispy Kreme long enough to wheeze his support. And Josh Whedon – whose only hope for consensual sex with a woman is pretending to be a feminist – also saw nothing wrong with a big-time feminist calling another woman a c*nt.

I can't define exactly why this particular word is so repulsive. Call me a "b*tch", or even a "ho," you will probably live to tell the tale. Though it's hard for me to imagine a more hilarious or less-successful "ho" than a small woman of late late middle age, in jeans, purple tennis shoes and a Second

Amendment t-shirt: "Hey, Big Boy, what caliber is your weapon?"

But, call me the "c-word," I may not be responsible for what comes next.

But, then, what does feminism tell women in general, but that we are NEVER responsible for our own decisions or behavior? Our icky husbands made us vote against Hillary! Blast-From-the-Past Gennifer Flowers screwed the Big Married Horndog for TWELVE YEARS, as a participant, not as a hostage, and just the other day she snatched (sorry) the opportunity to assert #MeToo status as a "victim". Woohoo! ANOTHER 15 minutes of fame!

The late, psychotic, plug-ugly dwarf Charles Manson shared his secret formula for getting a sizable harem of young women to do his bidding. Make them perform humiliating and deviant sex acts that break down all inhibitions and violate civilized norms. In no time, you will have a cult of lost, broken souls who are capable of slaughtering a 9-months pregnant woman. Yes, yes, I know that one person's "deviant" act is another's pleasure. I'm not talking about a wide range of "normal." I'm talking about violating all borders and boundaries of human decency.

Women publicly calling another woman vile names and men tittering about it instead of defending the slandered woman as a gentleman would is a marker on the steep slide to Perdition, a breakdown of civilized norms.

People who fret over the effect on "Gaia" Mother Earth from SUVs do not think for a minute about how fragile "civilization" can be. Civilizations have come and gone. If you not only separate sex from procreation, but even from loving intimacy, you have one ingredient for disaster. Demonizing normal, robust masculinity as "toxic" while unleashing enraged, unhinged, unfeminine women, immune to any criticism, is another way to hasten societal collapse.

I want to end by pointing out that virtually every one of these women in support of the use of the word c*nt were donning pussy hats and ranting about what a fiend Donald J. Trump was. If they believe there is an equivalence here, or that DJT "started" the War of the Vaginal Euphemisms, they are, as usual, not just wrong, but irretrievably stupid.

First, DJT's little decade-old exchange with the Bush boy was PRIVATE. It had to be dug up by the Democrats and broadcast far and wide. Second, the word "pussy" was not an epithet hurled AT anyone in public. And third, what he actually said was absolutely true: that very rich men have gold-digging women coming at them seven ways past Sunday and that the women are so shameless that they will even permit "grabbing them by the pussy." I have witnessed such behavior with my own eyes; ask any rich or famous man's wife how other women behave around her husband. To a certain kind of woman, wealth is catnip.

I will let you make your own pussy joke here. Shout out to our late friend, Jay Comeau, who died just about a year ago and is much missed. And Happy Father's Day to all the Daddies.

FECKLESS FEMI-NINNIES

June 22, 2018

Well, kids, it does pay to increase your Word Power. The witless Samantha Bee not only broke new ground by trotting out the c-word – and retained her wretched television show — but she modified it with the adjective that popped up on her Word-A-Day Calendar:

FECKLESS!

Not to be outdone, Kathy Griffin of bloody, severed head fame, pouted aloud why Mrs. Bee got to say naughty words and not lose her television show, when SHE, Kathy Griffin, lost her Squatty Potty spokes-gig just for doing her hilarious ISIS impression? With the head of the duly elected President of the United States dangling from her arm. And, then, she must have concluded that it had something to do with that magical, incantational word: feckless.

But Kathy could not call Ivanka a totally different, yet, equally disgusting name. That had already been done. So, she had to pick another Trump. She called Melania a "feckless POS." She assured us long ago that young Barron Trump will not be off limits for her rapier-like wit, so we can expect that soon a teenage boy will be a feckless "teabagger." At minimum. Sadly, "c*ck-holster" and several other great words have also already been taken. What's a weepy, unfunny, nasty attention whore with a Carter-era speed limit IQ to do?

These crude, hateful, degenerate women, chock full of feck though they be, have suddenly discovered that it is sad when children are separated from their parents. We won't even discuss the million babies scraped from their mothers' wombs yearly. We'll stick to the already born. How well I recall the tears of the femi-ninnies when Kate Steinle's dying words were a plea for her father to help her. Oh wait, I must be thinking of someone else. The children brutalized by MS-13, bless their divine-sparky little hearts, mourned by Nancy Pelosi.

In the Grotesque Comparison & Obscene Equivalency Olympics, there has been a competition in the last several days for who can offend sensibilities the most grievously. Are the children's shelters merely Japanese Internment Camps? (Laura Bush, my favorite First Lady ever, who should know better). Or are they just the same as Auschwitz? Ding, ding, ding! We have a winner!

As it happens, our extended family knows quite a bit about both. There will be nothing funny forthcoming here, though it is my stated mission. I'm sorry, but as the saying goes, "I can't even…" Maybe next week. After I clean the part of my keyboard where my head exploded.

My husband's family lost dozens of people to the Holocaust, including my husband's grandfather, his brothers, their wives and children. A few relatives survived the camps, and one climbed a fence to escape a transportation camp en route to Auschwitz. One of our cousins in Israel met a survivor who searched her out and who threw himself upon her sobbing. He explained that he was alive only because her uncle Latze (may his memory be for a blessing) had given him, then a child, all his food while Latze starved to death. Latze strung out his agonizing death as long as he could in order to keep his starvation rations coming so he could give them to children.

Now we also happen to know something about illegal alien children. In the early '90s, we took in a 13-year-old boy, Antonio, from Honduras who had, of course, been coached to request asylum. He was an orphaned street child in Tegucigalpa, Honduras, who had walked from Honduras to Mexico and crossed the Rio Grande at Brownsville. He turned himself in and was placed in the children's shelter. He referred to the shelter as the most wonderful home he had ever had before ours. They had classes, sports, lawyers, new clothes, food and a clean bed. Paid for by the terrible, racist American taxpayers. Feckless, every last one.

Do-gooder lefties from Minnesota, feckful to the max, went down to Texas to take six boys out who were waiting for their cases slowly to slog their way to court and brought them back to Minnesota to work on farms up north. Through a series of events too complicated to go into in this small space, Mr. AG wound up representing Antonio in court. He won asylum based on the fact that he is black. It turns out – though somehow you never hear about it – that beige and tan and brown Hondurans and Mexicans persecute and abuse black children. Go know.

We came to love him like a son and he lived with us for four years. Heart-warming story, nu? Ah, but alas, not the WHOLE story. He, like all of the "youths," had come with no papers and was encouraged to shave at least three years off his age. The younger the kid, the more sympathy he could draw and the longer before he would have to be "feckful" (responsible).

Tragically, he never achieved even partial feckibility. We lived through four years of drugs, gangs, glue sniffing, rehab, counseling, serious and accurate sexual harassment charges against him and more. Of the six boys brought into Minnesota by the do-gooders, one impregnated two different young women nearly simultaneously, one of whom had a preemie that cost the Medicare system over a million dollars. He was "separated" from the other little boy because he simply left the boy's mother. Several of the illegals just disappeared and never bothered to show up for any of their hearings. Some became criminals.

A second boy whom we helped, Pedro, an El Salvadoran who was the hardest-working young person I have ever seen, turned out great. He lost his asylum hearing but married a U.S. citizen, became a naturalized American citizen, moved to Florida and is a tax-paying over the road trucker, home owner, husband, and father of a very bright little girl who competes in STEM contests and projects. I figure America is batting about 1 for 6 on that batch of illegals. Multiplied by tens of thousands. If only we could straight up trade Lena and Kathy and Chelsea and Samantha, Bill Maher, and a femi-ninny to be named later for six Pedros.

I read that 80 percent of unaccompanied girls and women are raped. What kind of parents send their little girls out to "take one for the team" in order to win that great lottery – America — and all her largesse? The parents know the score when they commit the crime; the crocodile tears now being shed for being temporarily separated from their children are just an end-run ploy. If you want to cry for children separated from parents, hold a thought for military families.

Feckless Femi-ninny "comediennes": shut the feck up. Normal Americans are sick of you.

DIRTY THESAURUS

June 29, 2018

(Peter Fonda, the subject of the majority of this column, did pass away of lung cancer on August 16, 2019. He was a human being and evidently was mourned by several people. Nevertheless, I stand by every word in the column.)

Peter Fonda, 78-year-old "baby" brother of 80-year-old Hanoi Jane, is still alive! I had no idea. Boy, it is getting harder and harder for these great feminist men and their #MeToo womyns to come up with ever more disgusting slang for lady bits, hurled as insults at conservative women. But "Gash"? Seriously? Wow. I can't even think when I last heard that shocking word. But I know a hardened combat vet who says words I've never heard of, who would never even think of using it. He has a mother, sisters, a wife, women comrades and three daughters.

We also got a horrific little peek into the drug-addled fantasy life of this world-class Shakespearean actor. If the expression "rolling over in his grave" is accurate, Henry Fonda is probably now a new source of energy. Henry was a liberal, but best friends with Jimmy Stewart, who was a conservative. Haha! Remember those Quaint Olde Days? When people who disagreed politically did not call each other "Nazi" or "deplorable"?

Peter Fonda (or peter-fondler?) proudly and openly Tweeted his wish for a naked woman in stocks for random passersby to whip and poke at. Charmed, I'm sure. Oh, not done yet? And an adolescent Barron Trump locked in with pedophiles. Hey, genius, one of the main reasons why children ARE separated from adults in prison is precisely to prevent their being locked up with pedophiles.

Has creepy Peter Fonda done ANYTHING since *Easy Rider*? I hated that movie when I was a very young left-wing Democrat. In the unlikely event I ever watch it again, this time I will cheer for the Louisiana "rednecks" who shoot his drug dealing character.

Here's a couple of fun facts you might not be aware of about *Easy Rider* (besides the fact that they used real drugs in the movie): Actor Rip Torn was supposed to be in the film originally, but in a production meeting in New York with Dennis Hopper, Torn, a Texan, was offended by Hopper's bigoted remarks about Southern rednecks. He withdrew from the project. Furthermore, in a scene in a Louisiana restaurant where they used real locals, the people were TOLD that the characters played by Hopper and Fonda had raped and killed a local girl. The vitriol unleashed in the scene was, at least in part, a legitimate reaction to that misinformation rather than bigotry. But back to the present.

I understand Fonda has some new "indie" movie coming out. I can't wait to see the feminists knitting new "gash" hats to parade around preventing people from seeing it. Right? Right?

Remember a couple of weeks ago when I said that Mr. AG is constantly saying that "There is no bottom" to the antics of these unhinged leftists? He knows this; I know this; and yet we both go around with constant deer in headlights faces – like rich, vain women who have recently had "work" done – at each new travesty. I guess we either have a long learning curve, or way too much faith in our fellow man.

We keep expecting that some responsible adult Democrat – Joe Biden? Amy Klobuchar? Obama himself? — will step up and say, "OK, kids, dial it down. Not only is calling a woman 'c*nt' and 'gash' completely over-the-top unacceptable, but it's going to blow up in our faces."

Where are the grownups? The worst offenders among them are at least in their 40s and 50s and many are in their 60s and 70s. As Archie Bunker used to say: "Good Night, Nurse!"

Are there NO Democrats who are embarrassed by their spokes-cretins? When Robert De Niro taxed his tiny brain to come up with his fetching "F*ck Trump!" line, was there not a single theatre patron who would stay seated like a dignified, civilized adult, instead of jumping up like a functionary in an ill-fitting suit at a speech by Stalin? What kind of message would it have sent had there been no applause at all? It wouldn't have even taken boos to make the point, but just stunned silence. A presenter at a major televised awards show said "F*ck" the sitting President of the United States. Twice. And got a standing ovation. Let that sink in.

Remember when South Carolina congressman Joe Wilson rudely, if accurately, interrupted President Obama's State of the Union Address by yelling "You lie!"? OMG, the Wrath of Khan fell upon him. Mind-reading sensation Maureen Dowd "heard" the yuge no-no word "Boy" after "You lie." Charges of "raaaacism" were trumpeted across the land. No obscenity. No crude mention of Michelle's lady bits. Just rudeness. He was reprimanded by Congress and then overwhelmingly re-elected. By the way, I did not think it was either appropriate or good manners. And I easily disliked Obama as much as anyone dislikes Trump. But I am both sane and a courteous adult.

Ah, but that was in 2009. A virtual lifetime ago, politically. It is 2018, half-way through the year toward 2019. Now the naughty boy late-show hosts — Lord, how far we've fallen from Johnny Carson – and the small gaggle of crude, talentless women comics, are sent scurrying to their Dirty Thesauruses for new, ground-breaking territory every day.

I think tw*t and sn*tch are still available, kids. But they both are kind of "friendly" words, not really as reprehensible as the ones already taken. Have you thought of decapitation porn? Oh, wait, that's been done, too. Have you thought of acting like a mature, civilized adult?

Naaaah. Where's the money, attention, and insanely-lucrative series or comedy special in that? Look up the net worth of all of these obscene deranged clowns. It boggles the mind. Excuse me, now I have to get out my Urban Dictionary to see what combination of ugly words I can string together to get rich. Got my eye on an HBO Special called "F**k, f**k, f**k, you F**king F**kers!" (Hope I don't get sued for plagiarizing Keith Olbermann). I won't settle for a penny less than $50 million. With wit like that, I think I have a good shot! I'll take all my regular commenters out for dinner at The Bigoted Red Hen. ("Reservation for 500, please, in the armed section...") We will order the Surf 'N Turf, use the restrooms, forget to flush, and leave. Good for the goose; good for the Red Hen.

JULY, AUGUST, SEPTEMBER, 2018

If you are surprised that Crazy continues, you have not been paying attention. A workplace decrees that no employee may gaze upon another for more than 5 seconds lest that gazee feel unsafe.

This is followed by a piece about the wretched state of journalism today, which is followed by yet another trip from Arizona to Minnesota, this time because my poor Papa had fallen and broken seven ribs. I'm going to spare the reader any sadness or suspense by revealing that Daddy recovers completely, but there are no fewer than five columns over this quarter that deal with the crisis and the trip, including a heart-felt tribute to his caregivers and nurses in general.

A woman writer whose book was displayed in Walmart – "What To Tell Our Daughters About the 2016 Election" – is as upset over Hillary's defeat as I was delighted. I offer an alternative narrative of what to tell our daughters, despite the fact that I have none.

The theme continues in a way with a column about yet another journalist hatin' on the American people. Well, not all of them, of course, just what he calls "the garbage people". If you've bought this book, you could very well fall into that category, I'm sorry to say. Welcome to our world, my friend. We "garbage people", a variation on "white trash", are the last people in America someone can insult, denigrate, mischaracterize, possibly even beat up, and suffer no consequences.

The quarter ends with yet another of my trademark swipes at the vile #MeToo movement. There is no offense too minor, no human touch too brief, no passing pat too many decades ago to merit a few minutes in the spotlight. I hate everything about it.

NEW FIVE SECOND RULE

July 6, 2018

Every kid over the age of 2 knows about the "five second rule." You drop your candy or cookie on the floor, if it doesn't have any visible dust or hair on it, you are allowed to eat it, providing you yell out "Five second rule!" promptly. The yelling is critical. Like claiming "shotgun" in the family car. Or "Jinx, you owe me a Coke!" when you say the same thing as your friend.

Old habits die hard. The Five Second rule was good news for all of us who later found loose Certs and fuzzy Milk Duds in the bottoms of our purses. Though that often became the Five Month Rule.

This is one of the cases where the Overburdened Mothers of the 50s – who did not have just Taylor or Mackenzie to hover over, but Bobby, Joey, Susie, Sally, Kathy, and David — were both right and wrong. It turns out that the TIME on the floor – which has been walked on by filthy shoes, pets, and God knows what-all – is not the issue. The floor is absolutely covered with germs. That is indisputable. And now, your candy is, too. However, it also turns out that kids that are raised in a hothouse environment who are never exposed to these icky things never develop any resistance to any of it. So eating a dropped gumdrop OK; Mother boiling your Monopoly houses and hotels as my late, great Mama did – bad idea.

That was the old rule.

Netflix has a new five second rule: you may not look at another employee for over 5 seconds. As REM sang so long ago: "It's the end of the world as we know it." And then they added, of course, "and I feel fine."

I DO feel fine. I am not currently an employee and haven't been for about 40 years, give or take, counting 30 years in self-employment and around 10 retired. This is very lucky for me, because the next "Five Second Rule" would have been oddsmakers laying bets on the over/under of whether I could last more than 5 seconds in the new insane workplace.

I have referenced my "two years before the mast," working nightshift in a type shop as the only woman with 40 men and no management supervision. This was the late '70s. I was 31. One night I returned from the ladies' room to find an 8 x 10 photo on my typesetting station. It was just one of hundreds from the prized porno collection of an Italian immigrant named Mario. What was it, you ask? Let me just say that if Bill Clinton had been able to accomplish the truly remarkable contortionist feat of the lone man pictured, he would have had no need for Monica and possibly Hillary would be President today, perish the thought.

All eyes were on The New Grrrll. For more than 5 seconds, I'm pretty sure. "Aha," I thought, when I recovered from the sight of the photo. "This is a test. If I act at all upset, this will never end." I picked up the photo, handed it back to Mario and said, "You accidentally left a photo from your wedding night on my station." Yuge laughs. Grrrll passed test. That particular travesty never happened again. Can you see why I am not impressed when a crybaby goes to Spike, the Feminist Studies graduate, now the Corporate HR Intersectionality Drone, to report that Man-Bun Jaden in Accounting looked at her for 6 seconds?

Now I "hear" (intuit) two things: first, many of my women regulars and not a few of my gentlemen are thinking, "Whoa, AG, this really WAS pretty bad. Maybe we really do need rules for men who do not know how to behave?" Ah, but there's the rub, isn't it? Where do we draw the line? How do we get from Sexual Harassment meaning pinching a girl's bottom every time she walks by and leaving obscene photos on her keyboard to asking a woman out twice and being disappointed but polite when turned down?

And the second thing I can imagine my many fine gentlemen regulars are thinking: "WHERE THE HELL WAS MR. AG? HAD THAT BEEN MY WIFE, I WOULDA KILLED SOMEBODY!!" Point taken. And he would have, too, if he had known about most of it.

I chose not to spend my weekends riding the bus to Stillwater Prison to visit him, having had to sell the '68 Mercury with the bungee-fastened trunk to pay for legal fees. Plus, I'm pretty sure I would have lost my job if my husband had come in and greased the room. You know those highway signs: "Kill a road worker: $10,000 fine"? I think there was a sign in our lunchroom that said, "Your spouse kills more than one co-worker, kiss your job goodbye." Maybe not.

I had gone from $3.50 an hour as a secretary to $7.89 as an apprentice. On my way to $11.00/hour as a journeyman! To directly contradict billionaire Mrs. Pelosi's "crumbs" statement, that was a LIFE-ALTERING event for us. I served my apprenticeship, got my skills, my journeyman's card, and moved on. Grateful for the opportunity. We bought a house!

My new favorite musical group, The MonaLisa Twins, have a song called "Nothing Is In Vain." I have always believed this. Unbeknownst to me at the time, this nightshift experience also prepared me for the rough-and-tumble world of being a standup comic. After sparring nightly with these little dopes, a heckler in a comedy club was child's play.

Mr. AG pointed out the phenomenal disconnect and hypocrisy at Netflix. Just as Hollywood lobbies for gun control and could not sell 10% of its films without weapons in them, Netflix, Hollywood, Amazon, the whole lot of them, COUNT ON our staring at lovely young women far longer than 5 seconds, which is why they are so often either scantily- or not at all-clad. James Bond without his iconic Walther PPK .380 and beautiful women would have as much appeal as a Miss America contest without bathing suits or evening gowns. Oh wait…never mind; yeah, that's gonna work out great.

So how is the Five Second Rule at Netflix going to work? Will there be a counting device in multiple overhead cameras, like the "3 seconds in the lane" deal in basketball? Will there be a gentle reminder taser and then escalating taser strengths for each additional second?

I am not at all interested in looking at other ladies, except maybe to try to figure out HOW they do such nice makeup and hair when I cannot. And easily 99% of the men I have worked with are not as attractive as Mr. AG, so the problem of violating the Five Second Rule has never arisen for me. YOU try staring at Tom Arnold for 6 seconds, if you could even get him to hold still for that long.

FOLLOW UP QUESTIONS

July 13, 2018

My dear friend Angela is one of the best and most sensitive conversationalists I have ever known. She is a top-notch saleswoman who has mastered the art of talking to customers. Most of us aren't very good at even faking interest in what the other person is saying. As witty, cynical essayist, Fran Liebowitz, once said: There's no such thing as conversation. There's only talking and waiting to talk. Angela does not need to fake interest in others because she is GENUINELY interested. One of the elements of being a good conversationalist, she assures me, is the "Follow-up Question."

Let's say someone at a cocktail party ventured an opening conversational gambit with "I recently played golf at Pebble Beach." If your response is "That reminds me of the television program *The Flintstones* because their little baby was named Pebbles. Remember that? Did you know that …blah blah blah," you are probably a self-centered person and will soon find your potential conversation partner drifting off to find the Onion Dip and Pringles.

A better response would be The Follow-Up Question: "Oh! How interesting! What did you shoot?" or, "Tell me about the easiest and most challenging holes." Or, even, "How big are the pebbles? That doesn't sound like a very nice beach."

One time at a social event at our geezer community's Village Center, I sat next to a sweet lady who, I quickly learned, was Canadian. And not just because she pronounced the word "about" as "a-boot". At least she didn't have a detachable eyebrow that I noticed.

No, I learned where she was from because I asked. I waited for her to ask ME something about myself. It didn't happen. I asked about her children, their spouses, education and professions, her grandchildren, looked at pictures on her phone and commented approvingly, and asked where they liked to travel. I am not exaggerating for comedic effect: forty minutes went by with me basically interviewing her. Not one question came back to me! Now, I am lucky enough to have good friends, PLUS a weekly forum in which to yak about myself all I want, so it didn't so much bother me as amaze me. Why do I reference this?

In the broken world of journalism, stories come and stories go. The ones that endure – on and on and on and on, and also on – are the ones that advance whatever narrative currently fits the leftist agenda. The others go somewhere to die, perhaps that same nice farm where a couple of my childhood pets were sent (one dog and one duck). There are no follow-up questions because the answers would not promote the narrative.

How many "hate crimes" – poop swastikas, pulling off hijabs, rapes committed by comatose boys, banana peels in trees – turn out to have been committed by the alleged "victim" for attention, money, or both? When the non-crimes that don't even rise to the nothing-burger of a "micro-aggression" are exposed, we never again hear about the perpetrators or any consequences. No follow-up questions necessary.

Every human who's ever been in a relationship knows there is lying by commission and lying by omission. Jack and Pete go to a strip club for many expensive hours. They stop at Perkins for coffee on the way home. "Where have you been?" asks Pete's sweet wife, gently cradling the rolling pin. "Jack and I were just talking at Perkins," says Pete with a straight face. It's true. Pretty much. And so it is with "journalism." Many stories just die a-bornin, and people who don't surf the Net or watch Fox don't even know the story exists.

Remember that election we had in November of 2016? Sure, you do. If you don't, may I suggest watching many enjoyable highlights on YouTube. John had a great compilation a few days ago. But the long-faced, "objective" analysts on all those panels on all those channels made many grave predictions and pronouncements. One of the Obscenely-Paid Official Angry Black Guys – Van Jones I think – called the result a "whitelash." It was endlessly repeated. He could not explain how voting for a white GUY instead of an awful white WOMAN was racist, but he didn't have to. Nobody was going to argue with such a felicitous turn of phrase. Never mind that the original word was "back"- not "black"- lash, so the "pun" made no actual sense. It's racist to ask black people follow-up questions, which is why Obama never got any.

How's that racist economy chugging along, Van, old Commie, old 9/11 "Truther," old buddy? Any follow-up thoughts on black unemployment being the lowest EVAH? No way can the Black Caucus stand and cheer for THAT during the State of the Union Address. Is the wretched Bill Maher's fervent hope for a recession a "racist" statement? Oh, heck no. No amount of human suffering is more important than "getting" Donald J. Trump.

Remember the Case of the Terrified Jewish Nebbish who had to hire a plumber? (See my column of January 27, 2017 column "GET A GRIP.") Anybody followed up on whether or not gangs of Trump Plumbers in MAGA hats have attacked Ned Resnikoff yet? Carpenters or Painters with Southern accents stalking him? Why not? Where's the follow up on that preposterous, mortifying story? We Deplorables are responsible for his never feeling quite safe again. He said so. If all the commentary in all the world were ranked in order of stupidity, THAT would still win hands down. And, remember, *The View* and Joy Reid are included in that competition. So how's about we revisit Ned and see if he still needs Xanax to leave his home or to let a workman in the door?

And always, of course, with the "racist, racist, racist" themes. Has any kneeling moron millionaire been asked to articulate exactly what has changed in the black community with the election of Trump? Five hundred days on, are there even fewer unwed "fathers" (read: sperm donors) stepping up to the plate to care for their children? Even more gangstas killing each other and innocent bystanders?

Au contraire. More jobs. More brave black thinkers daring to challenge all the received knowledge from the likes of doddering race hustlers, Maxine Waters and Al Sharpton. It doesn't take much to create a seismic shift. A Kanye here; a Candace Owens there; Diamond and Silk. How many young African-Americans sporting the number "42" know that the late, great Jackie Robinson was a Republican? When the black electorate finally internalizes how badly it has been used by the Democrats, well, as Bob Dylan said, "A Hard Rain's Gonna Fall." And, speaking for both Minnesota and Arizona, we sure could use some rain.

CALL OF DUTY

July 20, 2018

So I'm lying on the pavement in the Prescott Residence Inn parking lot trying to copy numbers off my left front tire. There are many numbers on the tire and I don't know which ones are important, so I just write down all of them. The blazing Arizona sunshine is blinding me until I have that "aha" moment that I shared with Sir Isaac Newton, Archimedes, and other like-minded geniuses: "Wait a minute, these numbers are also on the other front tire and my back would be to the sun." It's insights like that that allowed human civilization to march forward. Eventually.

A terrified front desk clerk at the Prescott Residence Inn spies me lying on the pavement and runs out to inquire if I have fallen and can't get up. This is the kind of courtesy and concern extended to women of late, late middle age. No, but thanks for asking. When I explain what I am doing, she says confidently, "That's BOY'S work!" I couldn't agree more; but, my "boy" has told me that he thinks it would be good for me to do this myself. Always pushing me to be my best self – you just can't buy supportiveness like that.

At my last oil change, the eager beaver service guy told me that with over 53,000 miles logged on my 2012 Hyundai Sonata, the tires were not completely bald, but definitely "balding," as George Costanza insisted. He – the Hyundai guy, not George Costanza — recommended four new tires before too long, preferably right then. I should have listened.

But we always like to procrastinate, don't we? Especially when a nominal $916 is at stake.

In Prescott, I only drove across the street to Trader Joe's or about 6 blocks to the Walmart. Any journeys further than that, we took Mr. AG's car.

And then I got the call. My 93-year-old Daddy had fallen in the middle of the night somehow and broken seven ribs.

My dear baby brother, who lives in the Twin Cities, only has a full-time nursing job, a mother-in-law in declining health, four kids and six grandkids (all of them in four or five different forms of athletics that need watching), so you can see that he was simply too lazy to pitch in. Haha. I kid. He had already been back and forth to the St. Cloud Hospital and Alexandria several times. Oh, did I mention he also had pneumonia? The big baby…

And so, as per the 5th Commandment about "Honoring Your Father and Mother so your days will be long in the land," I made an emergency appointment to get the dang new tires on and took off as fast as I could get there. Which turned out to be pretty darn fast. Drove 700 miles the first day to Big Spring, Texas; the second day 960 miles to Ankeny, Iowa, and the last little tiny jaunt 400 miles from Iowa to my hotel in Alexandria.

Along the way, I had to pass a tractor-trailer with a pilot car fore and aft bearing signs saying "Wide Load." Boy, what a terrible job that would be driving that aft car. Like the old saying about the sled dogs: "If you aren't the lead dog, the scenery never changes." Imagine many hundred miles tailgating a huge rig and seeing nothing else. Mad props to you, whoever does this job! And what was on the tractor-trailer, you ask? A SAND COLORED TANK! In fact, there were three of them in a row! And I thought, "Oh. My. God. The Paranoid Texan has finally ordered a tank off Amazon. I bet he's going to get a snotty letter from the HOA if he leaves it in his driveway."

In the past when I have made the journey back to Minnesota from Arizona, I have tried to glean and share several overarching lessons. Like: America is unbelievably beautiful; or, men are extremely helpful; or, depending on the kindness of strangers is good for restoring your trust in your fellow man. And, Flyover Land is anything but.

This time, I will leave you dear readers with just a couple of micro-lessons.

One, as referenced, git 'er done promptly when something needs doing that could delay you in an emergency!

Two, do not wear new white jeans on a long car trip. I was drinking my fourth or fifth cup of coffee from my Adult Sippy Cup when I hit an unexpected bump and splashed coffee all over my white jacket and white jeans. At least it was tepid coffee and readily identifiable as coffee. Extremely ungood, but nothing compared to dripping a melted Dove Bar in the same general area, making me look like I had just had the world's worst accident. And causing people in Love's to wonder why that weird lady had a sweatshirt tied around her waist in front, on a 98 degree day. Oh well, I'll never see any of them again.

Who could have guessed that a Dove Bar left in a hot car would explode upon being opened? Who could have known that the little Mexican restaurant in Esperanza, TX would take 45 minutes to make 2 enchiladas while the Dove Bar dissolved in the hot car?

Third micro-lesson: When you see a sign that says "Deer – 15 miles" do not relax your vigilance after the odometer tells you 15 miles have passed. It turns out that deer do NOT have little GPS systems that will prevent them from straying one foot beyond that 15 mile limit. Much like "Gun-Free" Zones do not prevent criminals from bringing guns into that zone and using them. It was night and I had been driving for 16 hours and was very tired. But in all my coffee- and chocolate-stained alertness, I felt I could let my guard down a little beyond that 15-mile perimeter. Not half a mile further down the road, I saw a poor dead doe by the side of the highway. Which gave me quite the second wind.

A few miles later, I saw the best sign of this trip. We weary travelers were in roughly the 47th construction zone on Hwy 35North, in single file down a bumpy narrow corridor with orange cones on the left side and oncoming traffic just beyond them, and a concrete barrier on the right. And the sign said, "Do not pass." Good call. There was one of the few rules in my life that I felt no urge to violate, had it even been remotely possible.

So now I am in Alexandria supervising Daddy's rehab for two weeks. I am astonished and thrilled to report that I witnessed his Occupational Therapist give him a 30-point cognitive test on which he scored – wait for it – THIRTY!! Way to go, Daddy. Prayers welcome from any and all faith traditions for a complete recovery for him and safe travels home for your intrepid, if messy, columnist.

GO WEST YOUNG MAN (And when you hit West Texas, keep going!)

July 27, 2018

I was on my way from Arizona to Minnesota when I passed through Jeff Davis County in West Texas. I was astonished that it was still allowed to exist! Maybe those totalitarian idiots who would knock down and vandalize our history did not recognize the President of the Confederacy as "Jeff" without his full name. Pretty soon, it might just be JD County. Or maybe Texans simply will not put up with the Stalinist erasure of important people from their history. Yeah, probably that.

Jeff Davis aside, the county named after him looks to be as bleak as the surface of the moon. Texans, before you get your chaps in a wad, let me HASTEN to assure you that I love Texas. It held a mythic place in my childhood because of all the Westerns we kids of the 50s were raised on. (Never mind that many of those shows were shot in Arizona or on the backlots of studios in California. If they told me it was Texas, Texas it was.) If Arizona ever goes blue – though one could argue that with McCain and Flake as our Senators, it already has — I will move to Texas.

But COME ON!! The part of West Texas I noticed shortly after the Jeff Davis County sign had no recognizable (to me) plants, trees, shrubs, or anything that could possibly sustain life. Not even cactus! There were rocks and some of the rocks seemed to have made a concerted effort to form some sort of "buttes."

Now I'm a small-town Midwestern "town" kid, not even a farm kid. I recognize farming land, including several major crops. Corn, oats and wheat primarily, as well as cotton and mature flax which looks very pretty waving gently in the breeze. I sometimes pretend to recognize alfalfa and soybeans, but I wouldn't bet any ranch on it…, and I can point out many of your major farm animals, mostly because my baby brother had a Fisher-Price Farm as a toddler. This was not farm land.

If you (correctly) think I have a limited knowledge of farming, wait till you see how little I know about ranching! I do know that the Cartwrights spent most of their time out mending fences, when they weren't fighting townies resentful of their wealth, or courting women who were doomed to die by the end of the hour's episode. Even as a young romantic teenager, when I saw a pretty girl look interested in Little Joe or Adam, I would yell "NO! RUN!" at the television. We all do what we can. My dear late Mother used to pray for characters in the girlie-girl romance novels she read.

Anyway, I saw no fences in this part of Texas, but it's possible that some kind of grazing animal associated with ranching was wandering around in the buttes, possibly snacking on the smaller rocks.

And it really made me wonder about either the True Grit or the heat-induced delirium of the first settlers to this part of Texas.

"Okay, kids, your Mother says she cannot stand one more mile in the covered wagon, so here we shall settle. Look! There's a butte, which I shall call Johnson Butte after Grandpa Ishmael Johnson. Upon this butte, we will raise this family. Kids, in a few minutes, I'm going to go back 100 miles for some water, but while I'm gone, gather all the coyote scat you can find with which to build our first hut.

"Girls, see if you can't make some kind of jewelry out of the pebbles to sell to passing tourists; boys, help your mother run after some tumbleweeds – see her way off yonder? – to make a fire for her famous Armadillo and Gila Monster Stew. Little Ishmael, no one cares that you are a vegan. It's Armadillo or nothing, mister, unless there are still some Kale Chips in the bottom of the wagon. Some day, eating Paleo will be very cool and only pretentious lunatics, who have had their taste buds surgically removed, will eat kale.

"Kids, this may not look like much now, but in about 150 years, there will be a sign, 'Rest Stop – Vending Machines, no Restrooms'."

And so it came to pass that such a sign did appear, and people came from miles around for the Vending Machines. But they remembered to use the toilet before they left home.

And while we are on the subject of True Grit, I want to thank ALL OF YOU for your various prayers, good vibes, and general warm wishes for my father's healing. Happy to inform you that Daddy is working his rehab religiously – if, by religiously you mean invoking the Lord's name occasionally during obnoxious exercises — and recovering nicely. He will be going back to his Assisted Living unit in the next day or two.

And by this time next week – God willing – I will be back in my beloved Arizona, possibly taking the northern route on I-40 as a severe change of pace. Though not at all to avoid West Texas, as I am a yuge fan of Vending Machines. Plus, the Fort Worth Renaissance is a favorite hotel with some of my favorite people nearby, one of whom is a true Texas gentleman who would never let a weary lady grab a check! So, it's entirely possible that I will take the same old route where I know every hotel, restaurant, and pothole all the way. We'll see.

I also would like to thank the several dozen helpful men who told me in last week's comments to look on the inside of my car door for the specs on my tire size, or, failing that helpful hint, to take a picture of the tire with my cellphone and big it up enough at the dealer's that they can use that data. With the relentless repetitiveness of the advice, it will be a cold day in West Texas before I ever forget it again, fellas. Though lying on the pavement had its charms.

THE TRUMP ECONOMY IN THE HEARTLAND

August 3, 2018

This will be a purely anecdotal account. I am not an economist, nor do I play one on TV. For one thing, I'm not dead wrong most of the time, but that's another story, lookin' at YOU, Mr. Krugman.

As regular readers of this column know, I have spent more than half of July back in my hometown of Alexandria, Minnesota and have a week to go in August. I have been tending to issues around my elderly father's recent fall. Remember last week when I thought I was getting out on "early release"? Haha. That didn't happen. As I've quoted before, "Man plans; God laughs." God, as you know, has a keen sense of humor. How else to explain the more absurd and comic aspects of human reproduction, for instance?

Not only did Daddy not quite make the goals to get sprung from rehab – YOU see how great you are doing at 93! – but we had a second tragedy in the family with the sudden death of my dear sister-in-law's beloved mother. It is not easy to pull together a non-camo/t-shirt outfit appropriate for a Catholic funeral Mass, with only Walmart to choose from. Memo to self: at this stage of life, always carry a suitably somber black dress and heels wherever you go, even to the grocery store. Maybe just always wear one.

But back to my economic observations.

The little town of 6,000 souls I grew up in has more than doubled since I left, a fact that I sincerely hope is merely a happy coincidence. The downtown, which used to have dime stores and clothing stores, banks, hardware stores and four drugstores, one of which belonged to my father, is now mostly little tourist shops with antiques, knick-knacks and souvenirs. Everything else has spread out along the Highway, anchored on either side by Walmart and Target.

I have been back here countless times during various Administrations, and I have never seen anything like this: EVERY SINGLE BUSINESS – from Walmart to Target to Fleet Farm to Menard's to every fast food joint – no, really EVERY one – has HELP WANTED signs out! Construction projects abound, with robust young men in the same color shirts sharing my hotel, going out to sites early in the morning. Clearly, local labor cannot begin to fill all the slots. The parking lot has vehicles from Kentucky, Indiana, Tennessee, Illinois. Some, of course, could just be travelers like me, though leisure travelers do not tend to drive beat-up pickup trucks. I think there are many men who go where the work is.

What I suspect is happening is that the better-paying jobs are siphoning off the best, most-motivated workers, and the entry-level jobs are going begging. In any event, anyone who wanted a job could find one here.

Which brings up another sea change. At least a fourth of the employees in my hotel alone are African-American. And I'm not talking about housekeepers and janitors, who seem to be either white or Cambodian, but front-line desk personnel. When I grew up here, there was not one black person in the town. As I do my 10,000 daily steps in Walmart to get out of the humidity, I see many prosperous-looking Hispanic families and black families, and – it will follow as the day the night – intermarried families.

And isn't that wonderful? Ah, that good old "invisible hand" of the capitalist marketplace. No need for quotas and regulations and Obama's tedious scheme mandating that all housing meet rigorous quotas – just opportunity. If you build it, they will come. How great it will be for these working black families to escape the crime, the gangs and graffiti, the drugs and other pathologies, of bad neighborhoods to live in a small town environment. Real Hope and Change, not the false hope and blatant racism of "multicultural" quotas.

I have never seen a homeless person in Alexandria, which does not mean that none exist. The climate is hardly conducive to outdoor living and no way would the locals tolerate crapping in the street and discarded needles. But I was walking to my favorite restaurant and saw a young Mexican woman sitting on the grass directly in front of Taco Bell's "Hungry for work?" sign. She had a neat, hand-lettered sign that said in English, "Please have mercy. I have three children. Anything will help. God bless."

I stopped to talk with her. (Though I am far away, I can see Mr. AG slapping his forehead in dismay.) She had almost no English and my Spanish is only marginally better than her English. I pointed to the three closest fast-food places with giant "Help Wanted. All Shifts. All Positions!" signs. She said in the Spanglish we were trying to communicate in, "No tengo papers. Illegal." Ah. I saw no evidence of any children in the vicinity, let alone three. She never indicated that the tykes were in cages in Nazi Trump's Dreadful Children's Zoos.

But I did wonder how in God's name she got from Mexico all the way to Minnesota with three children, no papers, no money, no ability to speak the language – what in the world did she think would happen? And who wrote that sign for her? Definitely, she did not. I gave her a substantial sum of money, wished her "Vaya Con Dios" and hoped not to see her on the way back from the restaurant. I did not. In fact, I never saw her again. Maybe she was the Prophet Elijah and it was a test to see if I could show the mercy she had asked for.

And here we get to the crux of the issue of border security: I would bet there is not a single regular commenter who would be unwilling to help one, pathetic hard-luck case with a handout, a meal, some used clothes, something. It's been proven time and again that conservatives are more compassionate than leftists, who are mostly generous with other people's money. (Which is not to say that there are no generous liberals; of course, there are. I know many personally.) But can we, as a society, possibly support 25 million hard-luck cases? No, we clearly cannot.

And even if we could say, "Okay, just these 25 million and no more," we would have to cut off all the chain migrants, the tens of millions more who would risk everything to get in on the NEXT "final" amnesty and freebies while they waited. Because there is ALWAYS a "next" amnesty. For the vile, lying scoundrels who reflexively cry "racism," who assert that we don't want anyone "darker than a latte," hear me well. The issue is not what color our country will be, but whether or not we will have a country at all. Everyone with even half a brain knows that. In the history of the world, no country that survived has been borderless.

WHAT TO TELL OUR DAUGHTERS ABOUT THE ELECTION

August 10, 2018

I was browsing in Walmart's meager book department and chanced to spy a slim volume called *Madam President*. Bwahahaha!

I skimmed it in about 15 seconds. I am affirmatively uninterested in GENERAL in voting for someone simply on the basis of the color or shape of xer skin. Specifically, I was not interested in voting for THAT wretched woman.

Then I recalled all the shell-shocked women on the telly on election night 2016 agonizing about what they were going to tell their daughters in the morning. What could they say to little Madison or McKenzie about how this historic event — that they were promised was in the bag — had failed? And not by a slim margin, but bigly.

Why, no lesser expert on everything in the known world than Rachel Maddow had looked right into the camera on election night with her trademark snotty smirk and crowed that even if Donald Trump had his best night, his best night EVER, he would still lose! She had the colored map to prove it! Later on that evening, she said we were in Hell. Oh, dear. HOW could anyone that brilliant have been so wrong?

It has been over 500 days now, so I presume the saner caterwauling women have worked something out. (Blaming sexism; stupid white married women; Russian Facebook ads; "racists" who preferred a white man to a white woman. General Deplorables.)

The even more unhinged are still knitting pink caps and baying at the moon, carrying bloody severed heads, dropping trou and crapping in public, calling other women the bad "c"-word – you know, all the tried-and-true ways we have to convince other people that our viewpoint should have prevailed. All out of the playbook Wellstone Funeral 2.0. Keep it up, ninnies.

In the midst of such embarrassing hysteria, I was compelled to think about what I would have told a daughter about the 2016 election, had I been fortunate enough to have one. Of course, it would depend on her age. Age five or under, I think I would channel Dr. Seuss and friends:

Hand, hand, fingers thumb
Hillary thinks your Mommy's dumb
She called us lots of nasty names
And made a ton of crazy claims.
The voters kicked her in the rump,
(Hard to miss), and elected Trump!
We eat green eggs but never ham!
And the Israeli embassy's in Jerusa-lam!

You know, something like that. For older girls, it would have been an awesome teachable moment:

Well, honey, I know you've been told you should be disappointed. But here's what we've learned from this:

First of all, whatever gave you the impression that you were going to get everything you want in life? Because of a prolonged contrarian period (*The Idiot Years*) where I always seemed to be swimming against the current, out of 13 Presidential elections in which I have voted, my preferred candidate prevailed in exactly FIVE. Did you see ME screaming through the streets wearing a mask, smashing things? Did you see me sporting very poor facsimiles of lady bits upon my head? No, you didn't, and not just because you don't exist...

Secondly, dear daughter, never, never, never believe the polls. They are not there to reflect actual public opinion. They are there to SHAPE public opinion and mostly to convince you to give up because it's hopeless. Bullies always count on your not fighting back.

Hillary was never going to win. She lost to a black man whose only credential was the color of his skin and the ability to read off a Teleprompter; she lost to a whitish-orange man and if Cheech Marin ran against her, she would lose to a stoned brown man. This is not because of sexism. It is because Hillary was and is and always will be a terrible candidate and a worse person. A terrible woman candidate is NOT better than even a mediocre male one. Would you want a terrible pilot or surgeon just because she was a woman?

Just as the Reverend Doctor Martin Luther King articulated that skin color was secondary to the content of one's character, your father and I believe that the PLATFORM is far more important than the color or gender of the person representing that platform. We had many issues we cared about, but none more than the top four: border control of our great country; support for Israel; freedom of speech and religious expression; and the constitutional right to keep and bear arms.

Hillary was 0 for 4 on these and President Trump was 4 for 0. With the astonishing added bonus, that President Trump actually intended to fulfill those promises! Hillary was also for increased taxes, increased regulations, an activist Supreme Court, the global warming scam, and the right to kill babies up until the minute they are born. She couldn't even bring herself to assert that ALL Lives Matter, can you imagine?

The final takeaway lesson I have for you is this:

Visit Wisconsin. Even if you're not running for anything. The Dells are almost like Disneyland and the Packers are a fun team, and the people are friendly, if just a bit on the sturdy side. Just trust me. If you remember nothing else from this discussion: Visit Wisconsin.

Well, daughter, I'm glad we've had this little chat. Maybe in the next election, the Democrats will run a dream ticket of either Mad Max Waters and Crazy Eyes Socialist, who garnered 16,000 whole votes, or Hillary Has-Been and the pretty Jew-hating, brother-marrying, Muslim bigamist from Minnesota whose name I always forget. Madam President, here we come! My heart swells with gender pride at the very thought of any one of those four women running my life. I think I will begin drinking in proactive celebration as soon as I hit "Send."

WHO DO THESE PEOPLE THINK THEY ARE?

August 17, 2018

Here is a little secret from the comedy world, my friends. When comics get together, they rarely discuss the great gigs – the standing ovations, the necessity to take several minutes after one of your greatest bits for the audience to calm down so you can deliver the next line. I once did a Women's Wellness Event in Pueblo, Colorado in which I got FIVE standing ovations – three of them on jokes! But that's not what other comics care about. Every comic with a couple of years' experience has had great shows — what comics call "killing."

No, what comics talk about in private are the horrible gigs. What comics call "dying."

I had a 30-year career, maybe an average of 100 shows a year, with, perhaps, a dozen really dreadful gigs. I don't mean tepid audience response – lackluster nights happen — I mean where you want the floor to open up and swallow you whole. Where your whole life flashes before you and you wonder if you had stayed on at the type shop for the last 20 years, if you would almost be on days by now.

One of these dreadful shows was for a national convention in Minneapolis of on-camera "talent" from cable stations all over this great land. A more rude, arrogant, self-absorbed, group of people could not be assembled than that roomful of thin, pretty, vacant-eyed Teleprompter readers of both genders. All sporting good hair and capped white teeth. Not a single fattie or Helen Thomas gargoyle in the bunch.

The nightmare began with the terrible, impotent emcee trying to get the superstars to sit down and shut up. This was a thankless task, because THEY were so very important. THEY were the pretty and interesting ones in the room. Who were those nobodies standing in the wings with the temerity to believe they could entertain them?

So sensing the lack of respect for the upcoming entertainment, did the emcee, one of their members, try to defuse that by reading our prepared introductions listing our credentials? No, of course not. He LITERALLY introduced us "Okay now, calm down people. The local organizing committee for some reason has hired these two comics who nobody has ever heard of. Here's the first one — ." And then he brought up my opening act, my friend, Tom, a fairly new but talented and funny young comic.

The emcee sat down and immediately set the tone by loudly chatting with his seat-mate, his back to Tom. Can you even imagine anyone you know being this rude? The whole room erupted in more talking and determined ignoring of poor Tom. I'm still appalled.

These are the same kind of people who are intolerably imperious, demanding and rude to waitresses, hotel housekeeping staff, and retail clerks. Tom doggedly did his 20 minutes and, circumventing the emcee, introduced me himself. I got a semi-decent laugh with the first joke and perhaps the first ten tables in front stopped yakking and began to laugh, but it was still really tough sledding. There were people milling about, walking in front of me, chatting in standing groups. I did my time and ended thusly:

"You people were the rudest audience I have ever played. Had you listened to Tom, you would have enjoyed him. For those few of you who listened politely to me and responded, thank you, and I'm glad you enjoyed it. For those many others who did not enjoy us, because you could not bear to shut up, lest some other human have the spotlight for even a minute – tough shit, we got your money."

I did not do a mic drop. That wasn't a thing yet. Mics are expensive and I am not a brain-dead vandal. I rarely used vulgarity in my act. But, I'm not sorry. I hurried in tears to the parking lot of the event center, screeched my tires pulling out – and promptly got lost going home.

I include this story to assure you that these are exactly the same people who decide night after night what "is" and "is not" news. They aren't nearly as smart as the average farmer, nurse, plumber or PL commenter, but they now have one relentless, single-minded goal: to overturn the results of the 2016 election and destroy the presidency of a man who was elected by the Great Uncool Working People who Love America.

The hilarious patriot, Colonel Schlichter, is absolutely correct: THEY HATE US.

They try to disguise it, mostly by a good offense, accusing US of being the hateful ones (as commenter Mary Louise reminds us daily and quite accurately). But every once in a while, they really let the cat out of the cellophane bag. One such recent time was when Politico's Marc Caputo tweeted that at the Trump Rally if you "put all the garbage people together, you could make a full set of teeth." Oh, the cleverness, the wit!

I looked up Mr. Caputo's picture. He is reasonably good-looking. Two things stand out – he has a nice full head of hair and a set of beautiful white teeth, indicating "dental privilege," possibly including orthodontia. My husband's cousin by marriage has a full set of lovely implants that cost her over $100,000 in Los Angeles. It's remotely possible that the average Trump supporter does not have a couple of years' wages to spend on dental perfection.

I studied that picture of the mockers around Jim Acosta. The snotty little twerp claimed to be "scared" — ha! There was no undercurrent of violence, no brandished bike locks, no arson, only mockery, which these prima donnas hate much worse than violence. The crowd looked perfectly attractive to me. Do you know why Mr. Caputo could even SEE THEIR TEETH? Because they were not cowardly thugs wearing masks, that's why. But if their teeth WERE less than perfect, for some rich little frat boy political writer to make fun of poor people's teeth is as unseemly as a group of physicists mocking the intelligence of the mentally handicapped. Not a level playing field, Marky-Marc. You guys pretend to hate "disparity of outcome."

Will Mr. Caputo's career be as "kaput" as Roseanne's or Papa John's? Get serious!

THEY HATE US. These are insufferable, arrogant elitists: Obama, raised in privilege and private school in Hawaii, calls us intolerant, bitter clingers who hate The Other. The humorless, influence-peddling, ex-First Lady who runs a fraudulent charity, and gets a quarter mil for coughing through each secret corporate speech, calls us Deplorable. And now this little twit from Key West calls his fellow Americans "garbage people."

Explain, please, Mr. Caputo, what is a "garbage" person? Because it can't be what you pretended – that you were offended by Yellin' Jim Acosta being shouted at. You talk about KARMA. Now, personally, I don't like ANY speaker shouted down. If I don't like a speaker, I don't go to the event. I have never even booed at a sporting event. But, heck, you leftists LOVE it when speakers are shouted down. You LIVE to prevent free speech. Ask Milo or Ann Coulter or Candace Owens or Ben Shapiro.

Is a Garbage Person different from a "Deplorable"? If so, how? How about "vermin"? That term did quite well in Nazi Germany. You know what a "garbage" person is to the Caputos of the world? It is a person who refuses to fall to his knees in front of them in wonderment at their brilliance and entitlement to run our lives. For one glorious night in November, we uncool, unhip, garbagey taxpayers utterly forgot our place in the Great Pecking Order. Pull up YouTube once again for the awesome compilation of politicians, media morons and "celebrities" with Carter-era speed limit IQs intoning with rolled eyes and dripping condescension: "Trump will never be President." Makes my day every time.

The Paranoid Texan next door thinks that I am very ill-informed because I NEVER – and I really do mean NEVER – watch televised news, even local. That's why I am always surprised by the weather. But, see, I hold grudges, and these biased, bigoted, cowardly lemmings make me sick. We cut our cable, don't go to movies, have been done forever with the NFL for over two years. We used to watch all three games on Sunday, plus Monday and Thursday nights. We recently got rid of Netflix. Why would I contribute in any way to the obscene salaries of people who hate me? Why would you?

THE LONG AND WINDING ROAD

August 24, 2018

I love America and Americans – even the white ones who smell like wet dog and have bad teeth — and I especially love The Heartland. Still, there are only so many times – maybe 50? — you can go from I-35S in the Twin Cities to I-10W without feeling a profound sense of deja vu. Mr. AG favors turning west at OKCity on the I-40 to go to Flagstaff and then south to our Dusty Little Village. That route was spoiled for me when I drove it in my previous car, a 2002 Saturn filled to bursting with everything we needed for 5 months of wintering. The Saturn, never known for zippiness, complained bitterly in the Rockies, especially stuck behind an actual house! Yes, there's a practice evidently common in the region, of people taking their pre-fab homes out for a little spin. Maybe just trying to air them out from the wet dog smell.

So I was definitely in the market for a new route. Many regular Commenters had suggestions. And though I always let Mr. AG tell me how to vote, like all the married white women who caused Hillary to lose, I am stubbornly resistant to his routes. How to get from Alexandria, MN to Prescott, AZ while meeting my two non-negotiable demands for the route — no big cities and no rush hour traffic? This time, my whole trip would be on weekdays. I much prefer to start any road trip at 0 Dark 30 on a Saturday morning, but that was not how it worked out.

Even though I am severely dys-mapic (or map-lexic, if you prefer), I bought a beautiful new Road Atlas and studied it for days. My first thought was to go 100 miles north to Fargo and then continue on 94W to Billings, before turning south, possibly even catching sight of Commenter Par Excellence, Deborah. She lives SOMEWHERE in the great and also large state of Montana. I was not confident that I could find her. If, indeed, she even lived there – SOME people are not entirely truthful on the Internet, though I'm pretty sure Deb is.

Anyway, every male person I consulted, opened with the totally non-judgmental "What's the matter with you? Are you *&%$ crazy? Why would you go 100 miles NORTH to get south?"

Eventually, I consulted with my best friend's husband, Wayne the Wonder Planner, who claimed to have a route that could get me back to AZ in 1400 miles. He did revise that irrationally exuberant estimate upon reflection, but he also recommended an excellent opening leg of the trip. I was unaware that there was a two-lane highway – 29 – that went through many small towns in Minnesota along the spine of the state and eventually meandered into South Dakota, where I had one heart-stopping moment at a sign that said, "Toronto." How the hell did I get to Canada? Not that it would be beyond my ability to get that far off course. But, no, it was just a sweet little South Dakota town. Whew!

I LOVED 29South! Once you get used to an oncoming pickup or farm implement every 20 minutes, it was extremely relaxing, almost Zen-like with lakes, prosperous-looking farms (one with a yuge TRUMP banner on the barn), creeks, trees and many crops. Many. What crops? I have no idea. The only "crops" I know about are ladies' pants that are meant to hit just below calf-length, but which always fit me just fine as full-length pants.

But I am going to take a page from the "gun experts" who write or speak in favor of gun control. They don't know enough about guns to stick in a thimble, or wherever one might stick things, and I know a similar amount about farming. So I'm going to just go ahead and bloviate in a confident and arrogant manner, like they do, OK?

There was corn, of course, because who can't recognize corn? Then there was what I am pretty sure were soybeans. After that came field after field of stuff that might have been either carrots, or tobacco and something that looked like pineapple. Yeah, that surprised me, too. Is sorghum a thing? It sounds like a disease made up by dentists. And Alfalfa, which looked nothing like that kid in Our Gang short films. Maybe just stick with the generic, "crops."

In South Dakota, I passed by my people's old stompin' grounds in Hamlin County. At SDSU in Brookings, the claim shack, with which my ancestors staked their land claim, resides in a nice little museum there. It is smaller than my garage. How they managed to have FIVE children in such cramped quarters is surely a testament to the human sex drive. And I waved to Watertown, from whence our Power Line host, John H, was launched to the Ivy League, Law School, fame, and fortune, despite his humble beginnings in Flyover Land.

Daddy's delayed sendoff from Rehab altered my plans a bit, and put me right square in the middle of evening rush hour in Omaha, which turned out to be much worse than I would have guessed due to blinding rain. I hydroplaned on to Lincoln, Nebraska, stopped for a restless night, and awoke to four hours of dense fog all the way to North Platte. Surreal! If there were more crops – Beets? Wheat? Cilantro? — I couldn't see them.

And here was where I had mapped out the most cunning part of my route – a little Farm to Market road, 83S, which ran from North Platte, 350 miles to the unpleasantly named Liberal, Kansas. From there I picked up the 54West all the way to Tucumcari, New Mexico. On this route, you cross parts of Oklahoma and the Texas Panhandle, including the hometown of the Paranoid Texan next door, a town I thought he was making up. Along this route, you find feed lots with tens, maybe hundreds, of thousands of cattle. Cattle as far as the eye could see and the nose could smell. Which at least tamped down the wet dog smell from the white people that Sarah Jeong, Forensic Nasal Detective and brain-dead racist NYT Editorial Board Member, discussed on Twitter.

When I asked the desk clerk – Hispanic, not white, with no obvious damp canine odor — at my hotel in Tucumcari whether rush hour would cause any problem getting on the I-40W early in the morning, she tried gamely to be polite. But she could not contain her smirk. "Ma'am, there are 4700 people in Tucumcari, many of whom don't have cars. You'll be fine." Okie-dokie. Where was my rabbi who always said, "There are no stupid questions"? Evidently that's just a comforting thing one says to a moron who asks stupid questions.

The 40 is a major major truck route. I believe I have the only regular passenger car left in America. It was just me, 500,000 eighteen-wheelers leapfrogging each other across America at random, annoying intervals, and a steady stream of pickups all the way to Flagstaff. To be continued next week. Until then, be kind, and for God's sake, white people, don't forget to put in your bridgework and shower more often so you don't continue to embarrass our race.

It's the only race you can insult, root for its members to be killed, and still keep your job. It's nice there's still one.

AMMO GRRRLLINSKY'S RULES FOR JOURNALISTS

August 31, 2018

Saul Alinsky famously had his celebrated *Rules for Radicals*. He was a major destructive jackass and inspiration to such other unpleasant figures as domestic terrorist Bill "Guilty as hell, free as a bird" Ayers, Barack Hussein Obama, twice a terrible President; Hillary Clinton, NOT any kind of President ever; and numerous other America-hating community activists.

That's a funny word, "activist." The vast and overwhelmingly majority of "activists" I have known in my long and checkered career were about as "active" as an elderly domestic house cat. "Inert" would be more accurate, except when they were running their mouths.

Which they did at the drop of a hat. Remember, kids, college was a primitive affair back then. We didn't even have video games except for Pong. For entertainment, we often gathered in someone's room for what we called a "bull session." We solved the world's problems with all the acumen and experience that the average 18-22 year old poli sci or sociology major possesses. But we had to do something for fun. We had no phones on our persons or even in our rooms! Yes, if we got a phone call, the switchboard buzzed our room and we had to run down the hall to the phone booth, bodily remove whoever was idling there, and get the switchboard to send us the call. Then we had to churn our own butter!

We had neither porn nor "sexting." Since we had no phones or Internet, if we wanted to have even fumbling, inept second-base sex, we had to do it in person – can you imagine? — providing we could find a place. That's where the expression came from, "women need a reason for sex, men just need a place." And in the mid-'60s, with strict divisions between Women's and Men's Dorms, and large, stern House Mothers, finding a place was not as easy as it sounds. Ah, good times, good times. But, I digress…

I have been thinking quite a lot about the poor abused and maligned bawl-baby journalists. Who, in order to prove they were not biased, bigoted purveyors of leftist GroupThink, had a coordinated attack campaign of 350 op-eds and editorials on the same day. Man, you could not make that up…Well, color ME convinced!

You want to know why journalists are held in esteem in the slot between "stubborn jock itch" and "televised political ads in the week before any election"? Read and learn from Ammogrrrllinsky's new Rules for Journalists:

One: Any journalist inquiring about someone else's sex life must be hooked up to a very noisy polygraph machine while doing it. Before any questioning begins, the journalist must be asked, "Have you ever groped, touched, or thought about touching anyone not your lawfully wedded spouse? Remember, 30 years ago counts!" Also, "When in a committed relationship, have you ever had sex with anyone else or tried to?" When the bells, whistles and sirens the lying has set off finally cease, the journalist may interrogate his quarry.

Two: No stripper or hooker, no matter how comely, will be permitted to weigh in on any subject on television. Strippers and hookers do not just have sex for a living. That is only part of it; what they really do is LIE for a living. The strippers get men to buy $2.00 bottles of champagne for $100, and feign an interest in inebriated men until the money runs out. Except for pretend Republican politicians from Arizona and journalists, they are perhaps the least trustworthy humans on the planet. They do not have hearts of gold. Jesse Ventura claimed that the hookers at the Bunny Ranch gave him "freebies" because he was just so darn good. (Let me take a minute to compose myself here…Okay…nope, I need another minute…) Jesse: They were lying.

Three: The Party affiliation of each and every politician written about will appear in the first and every subsequent time the politician is referenced. The current system goes like this: "Hilda Hatemonger, R (South Dakota), was arrested yesterday for license tags which had expired a week earlier. Hilda, Republican Congresswoman for 22 years, claimed she had the tags in her Republican purse but had just forgotten to put them on. Hilda is a Republican." Versus, "Keith Ellison, who is black AND Muslim, is accused by an alt-right blogger of being a fan of gangstas and cop-killers on account of overwhelming evidence to that effect, including pictures. We have no idea whatsoever what party the Honorable Mr. Ellison is a member of, but if we do find out, it will be mentioned soon in paragraph 27, so you might want to stop reading now."

Four: Likewise, if anyone's income or net worth is mentioned, then EVERYONE'S income shall be mentioned, including the news-ninnies reading the story. Currently, several news stories will just willy-nilly throw in "billionaire" before or after the President's name, like it's a bad thing that he is rich. Let's let everyone know how astonishingly rich people can get with no discernible skills, work ethic or talent in this terrible country.

Example: "Rachel Maddow, net worth $20 million dollars, will interview Michael Moore (net worth before a recent divorce of $50 million dollars). Mr. Moore believes that his most recent crappy movie will finally bring down billionaire President Donald J. Trump. Unless, of course, Tom Arnold, net worth $30 million (only in America), beats him to the punch.

Omarosa, professional ingrate, net worth $3.5 million (what a country!) also promises she has tapes that will bring DJT down. Formerly predicted to bring down billionaire President Trump is Porn Queen Stormy Daniels, net worth a paltry $2 Million ("crumbs" to Nancy Pelosi, net worth just under $200 million dollars)."

Funny, I thought porn would pay a lot more than that. Memo to self: when considering a new career, give a thought to becoming a snotty MSNBC commentator or a rambling, incoherent Speaker of the House rather than A Late, Late Middle-Aged Porn Queen. But, just in case, I am trademarking the names Haboobs Haniels, Blizzard Baniels and Sleety Spaniels.

On a different note: to those commenters on Paul M's post Tuesday night who mentioned me as a fill-in Arizona Senator appointed by Governor Ducey, let me say that, while I am flattered and grateful for the confidence, you triggered an entire night's worth of nightmares. And – in case it comes up on a quiz show – it turns out it is flat-out ILLEGAL to punch a fellow Senator in the face. Who knew?

FROGGER, TRUE TALES FROM THE TRIP

September 7, 2018

Here, at last, is the final installment of my recent trip. So, I'm just under 100 miles away from my summer abode in Prescott, Arizona, after driving 1700 miles from Minnesota. I am exhausted, slightly anxious about my father's situation, and very lonesome for my husband.

But yet I am in a remarkably upbeat mood. Why? I have just stopped for lunch in Winslow, AZ at my favorite restaurant in the world, The Turquoise Room in the La Posada Inn, so Life is really really good. I am driving and cannot drink, but I can live with that. I am the cheapest date in the known world for alcohol consumption and if I were to have – God forbid – a martini or even a small glass of wine, and then attempt to navigate mountain roads, Power Line would soon be looking for a new Friday humorist.

I am pleasantly full on The Turquoise Room's Signature Soup – a lovely cream of corn and black bean, which are two separate, beautiful, colorful soups that they pour simultaneously into the same bowl so they remain separate, with a colorful border of some kind of spicy creamy garnish. I know without a doubt that if I tried to put two different soups into the same bowl that it would not work out at all. I am a pretty good cook. I have total confidence that I could make both soups, but the getting them into the same bowl part would be an epic fail and a quick sprint through Elizabeth Kubler Ross's 5 Stages of Grief.

I have also consumed some delightful Machaca Quesadilla appetizers and the Chocolate Caramel Warm Brownie with Vanilla Gelato and Whipped Cream, each well under 5000 calories apiece, certainly. What could that hurt for someone who had sat on her dead behind for 3 days, burning approximately 200 calories a day while blowing through 2-pound bags of Peanut M&Ms?

Anyway, there I am, with visions of the Brownie still dancing in my head for the 57 miles from Winslow to Flagstaff, when The Holy One, Blessed be He, decides He wants to play Frogger.

Let's start with blinding, torrential rain.

It's not as though the notorious I-17 (both South and North) aren't dangerous enough already. As the Paranoid Texan next door constantly reminds me, there have been something like 23 accidents in the recent period just from wrong-way drivers.

Now Mr. Darwin certainly knew a thing or two about Natural Selection and all that, but why do these specimens of pond scum in the gene pool have to take others with them? How stoned, drunk, texting, or stupid does one have to be to be going the WRONG WAY on a DIVIDED Interstate highway that is also a narrow mountain road? It's not like when you see a jackass coming at you, that you have a boatload of options. Take your chances on a head-on collision at the 85 mph that Arizonans prefer to go? — or head for the guardrail and plunge several hundred feet to a fiery death? Force = Mass times Acceleration could be one of those pesky Laws of Physics that the song "I fought the law and the law won" had in mind.

The rain is also a lot of fun when the veteran drivers who habitually navigate this stretch of highway do not understand the concept of "driving according to conditions." Naturally, they are mixed with the terrified elderly tourists from flat places like Kansas and Nebraska who are riding their brakes at 22 mph all the way down the mountain.

Which puts me in mind of one of my very favorite jokes variously attributed to Will Rogers or SNL's Jack Handey: "When I die, I hope I go in my sleep like my Grandpa…not screaming in terror like his passengers." Genius!

Did I mention the blinding rain? Oh, but we're not done yet.

It is possible that God is a James Taylor fan, especially of his song "Fire and Rain." Yes, there were also bizarre pockets of fire. And big electric signs every few miles saying, "Slow down! Thick smoke and fire in the area."

Then come the signs alerting you to the possibility of falling rock. Why not? Though there are never any helpful suggestions posted on these signs for what to do when those rocks do begin to fall. Again, simply swerving around them is not an option on the I-17.

Ah, but not to worry because you may already be killed by the unidentified antlered animals featured on yet more signs before you ever get to the deadly rocks. I do not know what animal it is supposed to be. It looks too large to be a garden variety deer. Possibly it is an elk; I don't think Arizona is thick with mooses. Or meese. It's possible that Ed Meese, former Attorney General, has retired here. He is probably old enough now to be wandering a highway.

By this time, I am very sorry that I did not have that drink. My windshield wipers can no way keep up with the rain. I am saying the 23rd Psalm at random intervals.

When, suddenly, the torrent stops, the sky opens up and the most beautiful sunshine streams through the lush forest foliage. As it happens, I am listening, once again, to my new favorite musical group, The MonaLisa Twins, and the lyric they are singing AT THAT VERY MOMENT is "There is sunshine. There is sunshine after rain. There is pleasure after pain. And nothing, nothing is in vain." Wow! You couldn't make that up if you tried.

By God's grace, I survived to the 89 and then the 69, another fun road with stoplights cleverly placed approximately every 40 feet. It was all I could do not to pull my Sig and say, "I have just survived fire, wind, rain, deadly assault rocks and possible moose. I'm tired, lonesome, and have to go to the bathroom. I am in a damn hurry to get home. GET OUT OF MY WAY!!"

But the gun stayed in my holster. Setting aside picky laws about brandishing a weapon and moral qualms about homicide, I know that dead motorists do not help the traffic flow at all. Plus, in this part of Arizona, there's a very good chance of return fire. And, come November, we're going to need all the Red State voters we can find. Especially that guy ahead of me with the bumper sticker, "I survived ASU without becoming a liberal." Good for you, kid. Better than I did in college.

ANGELS AMONG US

September 14, 2018

I have always understood that I would do very poorly in a barter economy. Should all of civilization go to hell, I don't see myself surviving by saying, "I will tell you three good jokes for that potato." And that was when I was a standup comic. A columnist would have even less leverage: "Here, read this. You might enjoy the occasional clever turn of phrase. Do you happen to have any food?"

But I am humbly pleased to report a few occasions on which audience members have come up to me after the show to share a very personal story of what that evening of laughter meant to them at that moment in their lives.

One was a woman who told me that her husband had taken his own life six months earlier – no note, no threats or previous attempts, no warning signs — and, until that evening, she had not laughed once in all that time.

Another concerned a prominent judge in The Twin Cities who had presided over the horrible trial of an evil and insane woman who had slowly abused her little adopted son to death. The judge's wife told me that he had seen photographs that even the jury was not allowed to see because they would have been too prejudicial. She spoke of his insomnia and depression during the long trial. The event at which I entertained the judge was an all-class reunion for Macalester College, and he finally was able to laugh heartily and let go of some of the stress. We probably don't give enough thought to the endless parade of misery, cruelty, and human suffering that judges and prosecutors see every day.

So we all do what we can to lighten the load of our fellow humans.

But this column is about nurses. They are truly angels among us.

Since I so recently spent over three weeks with my father in Rehab, surrounded by nurses, physical therapists and caregivers too numerous to memorize all of their names, this is much on my mind. Doctors, of course, are critical to the process of healing and recovery, but doctors are pretty much already regarded as demigods and accorded that level of respect. I am not for a moment suggesting that they haven't earned it or don't deserve it. I just want to put the focus on the ones responsible for the hourly hands-on ministrations and human touch.

Friends, I simply could not do it. Let us set aside the patients' expulsion of various bodily fluids that would send me walking briskly in the opposite direction and right out the door, never to be seen again. The matter-of-fact way these professionals handle accidents of all kinds with the goal of preserving whatever dignity is possible just blows my mind.

People in Rehab – mostly, but not exclusively, geriatric patients – are usually confused, miserable, and in pain. Not to mention, lonely, frightened and bored. My good friend Randy was in a motorcycle accident several years ago with multiple broken ribs and a punctured lung and he told me he begged the nurses to kill him. Thankfully, they did not comply but he said that time just hung there.

He would look at the clock and it would be 6:30 am and then he would look at it again in what he thought had been at least 4 hours, and it would be 6:36. There are only so many episodes of *Law and Order* that a person can watch without going insane. (Bonus spoiler: if a man who is a minor

character – in *Law and Order* or any other such program —
has a timid wife who is wearing a cross, he will turn out to be
the criminal. And at LEAST a wife-beater and an incestuous
pedophile. Count on it. But there is NO anti-Christian bias in
Hollywood. You would have to be a crazy alt-right bigot to
assert that.

There is slightly-less anti-Jewish prejudice in television
series. That is not because of lots of Jewish writers. No, it is
because, on television, Jews – at least observant ones —
simply do not exist.

Ah, but again I digress. Back to the celestial nurses. Our
family boasts two nurses. My brother, who our father never
fails to describe as "a male nurse," and my nephew's
beautiful wife. They both have the requisite compassion,
smarts, and sensitivity for the job, and my brother, a Navy
vet, also brings to the table considerable musculature handy
for lifting the modern-day 3XL patient.

I was astonished not just by the professional medical care
that was delivered – which presumably could in the future
mostly be done by robots – but by the human love, patience,
and compassion that went with it. Robots need not apply.

We are in a sad era where the healing human touch is
frowned upon, even actionable. At least in Alexandria, MN, I
can attest that people know better. Elderly patients who may
not have been hugged for some time are embraced, patted,
even kissed on the head. Needless to say, the nurses
exercise the discretion to know when it is welcome and when
it may not be. Do you have any idea how happy it made
Daddy to have a nurse walk into his room in the morning and
say, "Good Morning, Handsome!"? The chances are
vanishingly small that in 20 years, he will appear on
television with an even more grotesque Gloria Allred,
weeping about how demeaned he felt. And not just because
in 20 years he would be 113.

At the Care Conference which was held to determine whether Daddy could go back to his Assisted Living place or needed more Rehab to meet his goals, he and I (geezers age 93 and 71, give or take) sat there with five lovely young ladies who could have been our grandchildren and great-grandchildren, and who would decide his fate.

They did determine that he could use more Rehab to make sure he was safe to return to his previous residence. They wanted to be sure he wouldn't just fall again and have to return to Rehab. My father – remember my reporting his 30/30 on his cognitive test — then suggested that perhaps if he had KNOWN what the actual goals were, he might have had more success in reaching them. Point taken. After an awkward silence reflecting our disappointment in the verdict, one young nurse quietly asked my father, "Jim, do you have anything further to add?"

He looked around the room at this bevy of beauties and said, "Well… I'm single."

BAT GUANO CRAZY

September 21, 2018

I may have been one of the few who really enjoyed Cory Booker's Oscar-worthy Spartacus impression on his audition tape for Democrat Presidential Timber 2020. You know why? Because he's a guy, that's why. And I am sick to death of women cornering the market on crazy. It's downright embarrassing.

Let us begin by returning to Joy Behar and her "Trump is LITERALLY Hitler" histrionics. In the sage words of Inigo Montoya (Mandy Patinkin) in *The Princess Bride*, "You keep using that word, but I do not think it means what you think it means."

Dictionary def of Literally: "exactly, precisely, really, truly." If DJT were LITERALLY Hitler, he is remarkably energetic for 129. And praying at The Wall in Jerusalem, his new home for the American Embassy? What a lousy Hitler.

You notice that the wretched woman's program on which Behar pontificates is called *The View*. Not "A View" or "A Bunch of Diverse Views." Just THE View. This is the Word from On High concerning what women are told to think. Hard pass. Especially delivered by strident, arrogant, humorless, incredibly overpaid women whose main qualification seems to be that their IQs can be no larger than 1/3 of their weight. Who the hell WATCHES it? Who gives a rat's patootie what these left-wing mush-brains think about anything?

We turn now to Unfunny Mean Girl Kathy Griffin who thinks high humor is accessorizing with a bloody severed head of the Commander In Chief of the United States. Let us briefly review her many attempts at redemption: first she apologized tearfully. Okay, to err is human, to forgive, divine. But wait! There's more! Within minutes, she took back her apology and blamed DJT for "ruining" her. SHE was the victim here. Remember, kids, in Feminist Bizzaro World, men are all-powerful and women are Perpetual Victims who bear no responsibility for any consequences resulting from idiotic actions. Then, she said she was GLAD she had done it and would do other equally effective stunts, such as make fun of young Barron Trump.

Finally, she asserted nothing would have happened to a MALE who had himself photographed with a bloody severed head of the President. The last refuge of any disgraced member of a protected class nowadays is to hide behind xer Official Victim Status. (See: Williams, Serena; Spacey, Kevin; Brazile, Donna.)

Let me break it down for you, Ms. Griffin. Normal, sane people are not fans of beheading or the people who do it – Radical Muslims, serial killers, and cartel criminals. It is many degrees worse even than wishing for John Wilkes Booth to reappear (a popular, if unoriginal, Tweet), because it is uniquely personal and horrifying.

Normal, sane patriots may have differences with the President, but they don't like people who advocate – in front of our enemies – the murder of a fellow American, especially the President. I despise Barack Hussein Obama, but I would have felt exactly the same way had you carted around his severed head. It is outside the bounds of acceptable behavior or protest. Period. And had it been done by a man, nothing about that would change. Look at yourself in the photo. You look demented. Get help. And maybe a sammich.

And how would Ms. Griffin have fared with that stunt under LITERAL Hitler? Ah, how well I remember the sad tale of

Kati Von Griffinwurst, who carried a bloody severed head of Hitler around for well over seven minutes before she disappeared from the face of the earth. Unlike Ms. Griffin, she didn't live long enough to change her story multiple times.

And merrily we roll along to the Kavanaugh hearings where women once again scaled new heights of crazy. Rosie shrieks that "women are going to die!" Yes, dear, and men too. All of us. 100%. Sad. The older I get, the more likely it seems that my cunning childhood plan to be the first NOT to die may not work out. Cher tweeted that "our lives will never be the same." Did you know that with Kavanaugh on the court, this will be at least the 3rd or 4th Republican Administration in a row that we've been told was fixin' to outlaw birth control? Luckily, for Cher and me, short of Divine intervention, that ship has sailed. Ditto for her son, Chaz.

The loons seem to have temporarily abandoned the attractive pink lady bits hats for the orange Little House on the Prairie style dresses and bonnets. This represents the dystopian view of a very bad writer who has evidently never known an actual man. If she had, she would know that no man who had total control over women – except for members of The Religion of Peace and Genital Mutilation — would opt to cover women's bodies in shapeless orange.

Did *The Handmaid's Tale*'s author never watch an episode of *Star Trek*? In THAT future, even the ugliest female alien beings have scantily clad beautiful bodies. They might have massive facial scars, scales or outsized ears, but they are thin, shapely, and identifiable as hotties, generally sporting cleavage. Not an orange maxi-dress or silly bonnet in the bunch.

And what must the author think of our wimpy sex that we would quietly submit to such nonsense? We are AMERICAN women, tough from day one – crossing oceans, rivers, mountains and prairies, farming and ranching alongside our menfolk, bearing children, working in defense plants during wars, becoming doctors and lawyers and astronauts and soldiers, and, yes, I have met a real woman Indian chief.

I have been to Ladies' Day at the tactical range. Trying to stuff us into ugly orange dresses and bonnets is not going to sit well with that strapped-up group in tight jeans, boots or high heels, and – sometimes – ill-advised low-cut tops which look cute but are not practical with hot flying shell casings.

No mention of mentally unhinged women would be complete without Crazy Maxine Waters, whose incoherent babbling has been reduced lately to the single repeated mantra, "impeachment!" She has urged fellow leftists to get in the faces of Trump staff and supporters wherever and whenever the thugs might find them – restaurants, stores, gas stations.

I must advise her and her minions that a very bad place to be would be between me and brunch. Especially featuring Cornbread, Muffins, Cinnabuns or other Butter Delivery Systems. Don't say you weren't warned.

#COUNT ME OUT!

September 28, 2018

I think the #MeToo "Movement" is the most dangerous movement since the KKK, which it resembles with its mob mentality. And, I speak with total moral authority because I am a woman, whose every squeak and whine is, therefore, "credible." I can credibly accuse any male from my kindergarten, high school, college, or long-ago workplaces, of the most lurid crimes, with no corroboration or even dates of occurrence. They will be pronounced guilty by man-hating leftist women and their wussified, terrified, man-shaped consorts who are so generally-repulsive that their only chance at getting laid is to pretend to be "feminist."

Even after Tawana Brawley, and Mattress Girl, the Duke LaCrosse team accusers, and the fraternity gang rape that never happened, after every poop swastika and banana peel in a tree, all men and most women feel they HAVE to give an obligatory genuflection to "but, of course, the #MeToo movement is an important and wonderful thing." No. It is not.

It is a deadly cocktail of Professional Victimhood, Neo-Victorianism, the hysteria of the Salem Witch Trials and the certainty of being found guilty of the Stalinist Show Trials. No man is safe, no matter how many decades go by, from being accused of sexual crimes. It is the weaponization of the fantasies or distorted accounts of minor, unprovable, or consensual sexual incidents redefined later by unhinged women. Which is akin to giving razor blades to female rhesus monkeys who are on an experimental program of PCP and estrogen.

I think Al Franken is an obnoxious wanker, but I don't think any of his high crimes against #MeTooism rose to even the lowest level of sexual harassment, let alone assault. His hand drifted toward some nice bottoms during photo opportunities? Oh, puh-leeze! How were the photo seekers harmed by this in any way? Were they mute or paralyzed? Either tell him to move his hand, grab HIS fat ass, walk away in disgust, slap his face or get your damn picture made and move on. The real mystery is why you would want a picture with him.

So perhaps you are saying, "Oh, AG has clearly never been harassed. She doesn't know the horror, the decades of therapy necessary to recover." Ah, but, except for the therapy part, you would be wrong.

I wrote a column about my experience with a pedophile. I was nine years old. Unlike Ford, I remember the year, the month, the location, and the utter terror of its occurring in a boat with his threatening to throw me overboard if I told. Guess what? I told. Within the hour. I was believed and made to feel safe. The man was later convicted of molesting his grandchildren.

Moving right along, I have had two episodes with flashers, once while jogging around a lake in St. Paul. As cops will tell you, it is tough for women to provide accurate descriptions of a flasher. The shock of it all, combined with the focal point of one's vision, precludes facial recognition. In the jogging incident, as I ran past, I screamed some bad words and the guy came out of the bushes and kept yelling, "I'm sorry; I'm sorry" as I ran away as fast as I could. I suppose there's even a remote chance that he had had some kind of gastrointestinal emergency that required him to be naked from the waist down.

The closest I've come to real disaster was hitchhiking. Yeah, I know. Almost as stupid as getting blind drunk at a "party." We didn't have a car; we lived in Minnesota and I had to get from the campus to our apartment in 30 below zero weather.

Oh, I had some "rules" – never get in a car with more than one guy; never get in the back seat of a two-door — and on this occasion, I violated both. Did I mention it was 30 below zero? With wind?

The two college boys who stopped claimed to be going exactly where I needed to go. After a couple of blocks, the driver suggested that we should all go to his place for beer instead. Uh-oh. And I said, "Sorry, fellas, I'm married." "We don't care." "Guys, the reason I don't have the car tonight is because my husband has it for training at the Police Academy." They screeched to the curb and threw me out. I never hitchhiked again.

The great Dave Barry (paraphrasing now) has a piece of material about the different perceptions of husbands and wives to household cleanliness. He says that when a woman asks her husband to clean the bathroom because it is "filthy," the man will go in, look around, maybe swish out the sink and be done with it. It looks fine to him. That is because his "STANDARD" for what constitutes a "filthy" bathroom is a gas station men's room.

I have a pretty high threshold for what constitutes rape as well. A friend whose job required her to go to clients' homes to meet with them was kidnapped at knifepoint by a bogus client, tied naked to a tree in a secluded area, raped repeatedly, and eaten alive by mosquitoes. She managed to escape when her assailant went to get food. She ran to the nearest road and flagged down a startled male motorist who gave her his own shirt and took her to the hospital. I think that would qualify for what Whoopi termed "rape, rape." When the monster returned and discovered her gone, he killed himself, and is currently having brunch with Arafat and his less attractive and more anti-Semitic twin, Helen Thomas.

So forgive me if I am not impressed with an adult college woman too hammered to remember anything until six days of coaching 30 years after the unlikely incident. Or one who – if it happened at all and definitely not by Kavanaugh — was groped outside her clothes as a drunk teen by another drunk teen. That would be an example of NOT a rape. Is there a woman alive who never fended off a boy's grope? Then I feel sorry for you! I was a happy, willing participant in many a makeout session and didn't use or need alcohol to pretend it wasn't consensual. I only dated boys who, when I said, "THIS far, no further," respected that. Plus they knew my Dad.

The truly sickening thing – well, after the end of Statutes of Limitation, Presumption of Innocence, picky little things like Evidence – is that these lunatics don't really care a fig about women if they are assaulted by Democrats. In the case of Judge Kavanaugh, all the hysterics care about is stopping a man who might not support their right to kill unborn babies. That's it. All the rest is embarrassing psychodrama, character assassination, and a kind of mass psychosis that could lead a "comedian" to recommend public castration without trial. Nice. (See KKK above, Jimbo, you disgusting putz, they already thought of that.)

In the midterms any man of any color, and any woman with a husband, brother, father or son who does not vote Republican is a damn fool. Men: Somewhere in America there lurks a menopausal neurotic in therapy who remembers you took her to the drive-in in 1982. Or, you didn't, and she's still mad. Hope you kept an accurate calendar.

OCTOBER, NOVEMBER, DECEMBER, 2018

The Third Quarter of Ammo Grrrll Year finds us still in the throes of the Kavanaugh witch-hunt and the first two columns address various aspects of that travesty. On the plus side, it also marks the launch of my FIRST book, *Ammo Grrrll Hits the Target*, as well as Mr. AG (with the pen name Max Cossack) also launching HIS first book, *Khaybar, Minnesota*. "The family that writes books together, fights over who cooks together" is our motto. Thank God for Rosati's Pizza and Greek take-out.

Moving on into the end of the month, the column discusses the inherent dangers in following the advice of leftist morons who urge brave resistors to attack Trump supporters in restaurants and thrust their fingers into the diners' salads.

You thought we had reached maximum stupid, but the very next column addresses the wisdom of taking political advice from naked women, whose brave disrobing protests were all the rage for a few minutes in the autumn of 2018. In a breath of fresh air – because one can't go around with an exploded head ALL the time, the column applauds a new concept in school pictures: air brushing!　But, a couple of weeks later, we can't help but notice a heretofore unavailable job, a "Repulsi-can", defined as a "professional Republican attack dog in the media – only attacking OTHER Republicans!"

We end the quarter with a sentimental personal story about four generations of children to enjoy a nearly 100 year old playhouse and then a nightmare scenario where my email goes haywire and my umbilical cord to the wider world is severed for many hours!! I know – it was really really scary. I almost feel entitled – like every other "oppressed" person who has had a bad hair day – to hijack the sacred title of "survivor".

PARTIES, THEN AND NOW

October 5, 2018

I have been either affianced or married to Mr. AG since 1966, so I haven't really had a "date" for 52 years, give or take. Is it possible some things have changed in the high school and college social scene since then? (Haha – I'm kidding, of course).

Neither did I date much in high school until senior year. (Sadly, not for lack of hoping or trying.) I had numerous boy friends, as opposed to boyfriends. But the parties I went to were just close girlfriends sitting around in Bonnie and Heather's finished basement or out on Loretta's farm. We made boxed Chef Boyardee Pizzas, played records, talked about books, read *Mad Magazine* aloud, and discussed our hopes, dreams, and boys. Parents were always home. Always!

Never even once was there liquor at those gatherings and, if there had been, I would not have had any. Except for a couple of glugs of cheap wine at our very casual wedding reception, my first drink was on my 21st birthday when my young husband ordered me Crème de Menthe over ice cream. Queen of the Nerds, huh?

Now I know that there were cooler kids – athletes and cheerleaders and the like – who spoke of parties, but these were overwhelmingly couples affairs. From second-hand reports, I gleaned that everybody paired off, danced, and snuck into dimly-lit corners to make out. So I'm going to go out on a limb here and suggest that even if alcohol had been involved, the girls would have noticed if a queue had formed with their steady boyfriends waiting their turn to rape. The very thought boggles the mind.

I'm sure I'm not the only one who has noticed that in the preposterous claims and anonymous letters accusing Judge Kavanaugh there has been a staged ESCALATION from one drunk teen groping a fully clothed other drunk teen while his wingman "laughed"; to weenie-wagging in a large group; to multiple gang rape parties and now, a rape-a-thon car ride story that was so absurd it actually made me LAUGH. And ALL missed by the previous six FBI investigations!

But returning to the accusation that started it all, to me, the most "un"-credible claim in Dr. Ford's unsubstantiated tale is that she got "assaulted" because she went upstairs to use the bathroom. Two miscreants were just lurking there, hoping that Nature would call one of the two only girls. There is no house in America without a bathroom on the first floor, though many do not have bedrooms down there. But, see, the fabulists had to get her to a bedroom to make this work.

The evil liars churning out these fantasies have obviously got subscriptions to Penthouse Forum. It has long been my impression that "rape" is mostly a solo gig. Yet in every fictional incident involving young Kavanaugh he seems to have chosen to have a witness along for the ride. Did no one else find this curious? Why is that?

Is it because two guys (or a queue of guys at the Rape Parties) make it more unlikely that the poor drunk damsel could not just knee the pig and escape? I guarantee you that at 15, even IF a drunk fellow laid on top of me while using both hands to try to disrobe me (not easy while lying on TOP of someone – try it!) AND held his third hand over my mouth while turning up the stereo with his foot, there would have been some serious signs of a struggle upon his person. Had I not told MY parents, HIS parents would have wondered where the scratches, bites, bloody nose and black eye came from. If he could still walk.

Friends, I can't take much more. So, this is me screaming in all caps to all and sundry: NO NO NO NO. Her story is NOT "credible." It is not brave or sad. It didn't happen — only with someone else. It is preposterous! And it is a tightly plotted Agatha Christie novel compared to the subsequent accusations.

But it does raise the question in both of the high school claims: WHERE THE HELL WERE ALL THE PARENTS??? Especially in the absurd porn fantasy told by Creepy Porn Lawyer's client. That tale included TEN, count 'em, TEN drug, liquor and GANG RAPE parties. What I love most about that crock o' kaka is that the college-age Julie loon either continued going to high school parties AFTER she had been raped or went back at least nine times until she finally got her turn. You betcha. Happens all the time.

One crucial mystery in this whole surreal, depressing saga remains unsolved: So please bow your heads with me now as we pray: "Oh, Lord, please let America find a Forensics Fart Slang Expert for the Kavanaugh yearbook. It may be too much for the FBI and fall to the CIA to solve. Lord, should we reinstate Brennan? It's probably right in his wheelhouse. He looks perpetually furious and red-faced such that he could have been suppressing painful gas for decades. Which would explain a lot. Thy will be done." Amen.

For the lying liars to have the slightest hope of their many fairy tales passing muster, parties must have changed dramatically between the '60s and the '80s. For psychotic partisan hacks who recommend mass castration, the stories don't have to make sense. But what about Normal Americans? What would make anyone say, "Well, that probably happened!"?

Certainly in that 20 years from the '60s to the '80s, fear of pregnancy at some point was not even a fleeting anxiety –

readily available birth control, unlimited abortion and lack of stigma about unwed motherhood meant every day was Christmas for horny young men.

Divorce became far more common. Did the breakdown of the family in the same period contribute to the opportunities afforded teens to get into trouble? Was it more common for children of divorce to be unsupervised or for a non-custodial parent to be kept in the dark? Or did rich, private school kids' parents travel a lot and leave teens home alone? How else to explain where all the empty houses full of liquor came from? With no nosy neighbors!

And that's my final point. I'm just a small-town girl. Everybody knew everybody else's kids and cars. Maybe neighborhoods with palatial, gated estates provide privacy for criminality. Let's say Mama and Daddy had been out playing several rubbers of Bridge with friends. So I quickly invited one girl and four guys to come over — pretty good odds, even for me – AND found somewhere to stash my tattletale younger siblings. Mrs. Saiko and Mrs. Wendt across the street would have TOLD my parents the second they got home.

"Sorry it's after midnight, Dorothy, but I thought you should know that Susan had quite a few friends over while you were gone… QUITE a few…mostly boys, too!" And being interrogated by Daddy would have been far worse than by Fossil Feinstein, Da Nang Dick or Departacus.

BIDDING ADIEU TO #METOO plus SOME COOL SURPRISES

October 12, 2018

To my certain knowledge, the only time in my life I have ever said, "MeToo!" was when someone asked, "Who wants cake and ice cream?" and someone else had already answered "Me!" first.

I'm just not a "MeToo" kinda grrrll. I have a yuge anti-authoritarian streak and a visceral, DNA-level hatred for piling on and going along with the crowd. You want to see "MeToo" in action, watch an old film clip of a Hitler rally, or (if you can stand it, and I can't) a picnicking crowd at a lynching. From the time I was a young girl, seeing those mobs that had surrendered their humanity gave me the same feeling expressed by Mark Twain, "Sometimes when you observe the human race, it does seem a pity that Noah and his party didn't miss the boat."

I have always feared mobs, maybe because I am so small, can't see over them, and fear being trampled. As over-the-moon ecstatic as I was when the 1987 Minnesota Twins won the World Series, I did NOT attend the gigantic parade downtown, rumored to be a million strong. I watched on television and enjoyed a sammich in the peace of my own family room.

Now when I wrote my last couple of columns about the mob mentality of #MeToo, I referred to some assaults or near-assaults that happened to me. But I hope you notice, I didn't name anybody. Of course I know the name of the monster who violated my innocence as a little 9-year-old girl. He was known to me, which is why I trusted him at all. He and his wife are long dead. He was eventually arrested for molesting his own grandchildren. How would I be doing the world a favor to use his name and smear and mortify his poor son, who would be in his late 70s now, if alive, or re-victimize the grandchildren?

I think of several bewildered and hurt actors — left-wing putzes though they be — who thought they were bantering and joking around with women friends from TEN, TWENTY, THIRTY, FLIPPIN' YEARS AGO, and now are "outed" as "harassers." Good Lord! Or Ben Affleck – multiple times named as "Sexiest Man Alive" by People Magazine – being accused of copping a feel from ONE actress whose outfit without a doubt was displaying the merchandise in an enticing manner. ONE! With all that opportunity!

Well, enough already about #MeToo for the time being. It's been edifying, but completely exhausting watching the p*ssy-hat loons, the Democrat smear machine, and their willing accomplices in the media go bonkers. But the good guys won. Again! We've gone from the 2016 Cubs World Series win (for Mr. AG), to the mind-boggling defeat of Hillary "No Civility; No Peace" Clinton, and elevation of DJT to the highest office in the land; to this Democrat swan dive into the sewer from which we eventually surfaced, showered off, and as others have said, celebrated with beer!

We need to take a victory lap, breathe deeply, gird our loins or anything else that needs girding, and relax however briefly before coming out swinging for the mid-terms. There is way more to life than endless political crap. So here are some relaxing ideas and opportunities!

Regular commenter Daniel Schwartz has a Barbershop Quartet CD out just in time for the holidays. It's called "From the Hearth." He mailed it to me as a gift, with no thought of asking for a plug. But it's terrific, uplifting music! I defy anyone to be depressed while listening to Barbershop – its harmonies are healing medicine. There are songs for

Christmas, Chanukah, lullabies, hymns, love songs. Their outstanding quartet made a "clean sweep" of the 2017 Boston Regional Harmony Sweepstakes Festival, taking overall Champions, Audience Favorite, and Best Male Soloist Awards. The harmonies are tight as an Eagles song. Order on-line here.

In our building crescendo of excitement, next I must tell you that my very own Mr. AG has written his first novel! It's a thriller wherein an ordinary small-town Northern Minnesota guy – WITHOUT the mad skill set of a Liam Neesen in *Taken* – must stop a terrorist attack. My husband has elected to write under a pseudonym, so look on Amazon for *Khaybar, Minnesota* by Max Cossack. It is $3.99 for an e-book and just $9.99 for the paperback. Now, okay, he's my husband so how objective could I be, right? But, I will promise you I was astonished at how good it is. Especially for a first novel. His characters are interesting, quirky and brave. And, ladies, he writes really smart, funny, strong women characters too, even an attractive Jewish, uh, ex-wife (should I be worried?)

So, please, friends, family and fans keep these three little words in mind: BUY IN BULK. Makes a great stocking-stuffer. Ammo Grrrll – who keyboards her sometimes-arthritic little fingers to the bone week after week for free — thanks you for ordering it today. And reviewing it on Amazon with at least five stars.

And FINALLY, numerous Commenters have begged for a compilation book of AG columns. One reader even suggested that I will be called to answer for not doing so at the Pearly Gates. Well, that persuasive argument seemed to get me off my lazy duff to compile Volume 1 of *Ammo Grrrll Hits the Target*, columns from 2014, which will include some additional never-before-seen material. There eventually will be 3 subsequent volumes! Start now to budget for the whole set!! ($20 for one, $70 for 2, $150 for the complete set. Hoho. Remember, ladies, Math is Hard! I kid. I kid!) Get a set for every bathroom in your home. Seriously, it will be attractively priced and Volume 1 will be out by Black Friday on Amazon.

NOTHING SOCIAL ABOUT IT

October 19, 2018

Generally speaking, putting the word "social" in front of anything either renders it meaningless or changes it into its opposite. Sometimes, like "social disease," it is just a euphemism. At any rate, I submit several examples of the uses of "social" for your consideration:

Let's just skim the surface of the worst of all, though it alone could be a 12-part series – Social Justice. Regular old garden-variety Justice – you remember the chick with the blindfold over her eyes? – was accomplished first with the Constitution and the Bill of Rights and then continued with the Civil Rights Act, Title IX, and the usual legislative and judicial channels for righting ancient and very real wrongs. For about 15 minutes, aggrieved groups were satisfied. But certain pathologies seemed remarkably resistant to eradication even with legal impediments removed.

Why, clearly MORE had to be done. It's not enough to be allowed into college, if it requires studying and hard work to pass the entrance exams. That gives an unfair advantage to…uh…those who study and work hard. Let's lift that blindfold just a bit and give 400 extra points to those who did neither. Had that blatant discrimination been confined to academia where no real harm could be done by a mental midget majoring in Sociology or Interpretive Feminist Dance, all might have been well. (And I say that as a Sociology major.)

But there were a lot of jobs that paid well whose troublesome requirements could actually impact on life and safety. If firefighters are required to hoist 200 lbs. of chain a hundred feet to simulate the dead weight of a person being carried out of a fire — and no women can do that — then we must figure out how few pounds it takes to guarantee that SOMEBODY without testosterone qualifies. That is Social Justice and we will never learn if people have died because of it. What matters is to get a Somali Muslim cop, or a woman Navy Seal. (IF a woman can meet the real standards for firefighter or Seal training, then I bow low to her.)

Social Media: It's possible that when dweeby Mr. Zuckerberg came up with the idea of Facebook, he genuinely thought "What a great way for families and friends to keep in touch!" Alas, through several incarnations of MySpace, Facebook and the like, we now see whole families out for dinner, not interacting with each other for even a minute, all hunched over their individual phones. I keep reading that texting drivers are more dangerous than drunk ones.

Social media is now used to summon flash mobs for havoc; it is used to shame teens into suicide and to make sure that anyone who steps outside the ever narrower Straits of Political Correctness never works again. It can magnify the most offhand, casual joke into a firestorm of hatred in a trice. What part of that is "social" or beneficial is beyond me.

Social Studies – I shudder to think what subject matter passes for Social Studies today, but when I was in fourth grade we had an over-sized Social Studies book devoted to other cultures. Two units that I recall from some 63 years ago involved "Juan," whose father was a burro-riding coffee grower in Colombia and – I am not making this up – Pimwe, the Jungle Boy, who lived somewhere vague in Africa. His mother spent her days pounding cassava roots into a flour for bread.

I do not remember what Pimwe did, because that big brown book was a perfect size for hiding smaller books, like the now banned Laura Ingalls Wilder books, inside of it. I hate Political Correctness with the white hot heat of a thousand suns. However, it is remotely possible that there were SOME cultural insensitivities that wanted correction.

Social Dancing in 7th Grade gym was not very social either. The unit went on for half a quarter. The scratchy vinyl record would start – the box waltz, a foxtrot — one of the long-outdated dances we had plodded to mechanically for a couple of weeks without partners (step, two, three, back two three…). Time to try it in pairs. The girls were lined up on one side of the gym and the boys on the other. The music began. And…nothing.

The boys – 12 years old, at the very peak of fragrant obnoxiousness – would simply not go across No-Man's Land to ask a girl to dance. Short of whips – which, surprisingly, were illegal in middle school even in the '50s – they just flat-out refused. The boy's gym teacher tried collective punishment. The boys could choose between asking a girl to dance and running laps around the gym. To a boy, they chose the laps. We girls danced with each other, free from the anxiety of waiting for some little punk to gift us with his invitation to bunny hop.

By eighth grade, more of the boy critters were now taller than the girls and in the grip of powerful hormones. They were awash in the '50s version of Ax Body Wash and, noticing that many girls had filled out nicely, they were now eager to dance. The same little fella sprinted across the gym floor every week to seek me out, never saying another word after asking me to dance. Finally, in about week six, sweating profusely, he came up with an inspired ice-breaker: "So…what page are you on in Math?"

I answered honestly, "I don't know the page. Multiplying Fractions, I think." He persisted. "Okay. Want to go to the school dance with me next Friday night?" "Sure. Thanks." By that time we had utterly lost the beat. And then his big finish,

"What's your name and could you write down where you live? My Mom will drive us."

That relationship did not even survive the evening. It was a disaster from the moment he opened his mother's passenger door for me and then got in first. Let's mention also that my Ban roll-on deodorant, when activated by perspiration, turned the armpits in my lovely new green satin dress, bright yellow. It's only been 59 years, so I'm almost over that part.

The evening ended at about 8:30 with the fight my diminutive date got into with another boy who asked for one dance. From the principal's office, the chaperones called his mother to bring a blood-free shirt and fetch him. I called my Daddy to come get me and bring a sweater to cover up my dress. I'm pretty sure my date grazed my behind once in a slow dance. So he probably can no longer be considered for The Supreme Court by grandstanding sleazebuckets whose august body has a hefty and super-secret taxpayer-funded slush fund to pay off sexual harassment charges filed long after junior high.

FINGER FOOD

October 26, 2018

As most people probably know by now, one James Thomas, Assistant Professor of Sociology at Ole Miss, advised: "Don't just interrupt a Senator's meal, y'all. Put your whole damn fingers in their salads. Take their apps and distribute them to the other diners. Bring boxes and take their food home with you on the way out. They don't deserve your civility."

Wow! I know The South has some problematic history, but I thought we could always count on it for exquisite manners. Who knew "civility" had to be merited – not even by how one treats others, but by one's opinions? And who shall be the Head Arbiter of Merited Civility? Hillary? Mad Max? Professor Thomas himself? Evidently.

This paragon of moral rectitude and scholarship (Sociology? Really? That's even still a major?) who has undue influence over impressionable (and grade-grubbing) students, has not been fired for advocating several major felonies in the name of "Democratic" Socialist activism. There's felonious assault, of course, and then premeditated theft, and probably several OSHA violations what with sticking fingers that have been God knows where into a diner's meal.

You know what I would LOVE to be able to do? (Besides bring back to life a pioneer family that took six months to get from St. Joe, Missouri to California in a covered wagon, and put them in First Class for a flight of two-three hours across the same territory. Wouldn't THAT be a hoot?) I would love to bring back JFK, Democrat icon par excellence, and show him what his Party has become. I bet the first thing he'd do is slap his moron third-generation relatives silly.

"Guess what, Mr. President? Remember when you were devastated and laid low over losing your little baby, Patrick Bouvier Kennedy, who was five weeks premature? Your Party advocates the 'right' of women to kill their babies at Patrick's age and right up to the minute they are no longer in their mother's body. No, really, I'm not making that up. Women take out full-page ads in the newspaper bragging that they have done that. A D-Level actress and relentless attention addict named Lena bemoans the fact that she's never had the opportunity to kill a baby. Here's her picture. Yes, sir, I agree that she definitely is 'no Marilyn,' even without the silly tattoo and extra 50 pounds.

"There's more, Mr. President. Remember how you were all but worshipped by the Black community for advocating for basic human and civil rights for all? Now, activists in that same community and the entire Democrat leadership, including its standard-bearer in the last election, steadfastly refuse to say that 'ALL Lives Matter.' You can look it up. Normal Black people disagree, of course, as do normal people of all colors.

"I'm afraid we're not done yet. A jackass professor at Ole Miss has incited others to assault U.S. Senators in restaurants, and – try not to gag, sir – 'stick their fingers into their salads' before boxing them up to give to others, possibly the homeless, who enjoy a good used salad."

"Yes, the cowardly masked thugs setting things on fire and hitting pedestrians with bike locks in this video are Democrats or far-left fans of totalitarianism who will vote Democrat anyway. They probably just like destroying things and hurting people, but they claim to be fighting to get everything free – college, health care, so forth. Yes, I know, you spoke brilliantly of asking not what our country could do for us, but what we could do for our country. That message implied that people were responsible for their own lives, but since that useless Commie killed you, we have learned that almost everyone is just a pathetic, entitled victim. Not you, sir, of course, you are a rich white man reputed to like women, unless that was just a rumor, so pretty much everything is your fault.

"You want to go back to where you were resting in peace? Who could blame you?"

Usually, when I read something as stupid and evil as what Assistant Professor Thomas advocates, it makes me angry. But sometimes it just makes me sad. Who ARE these fellow Americans who cannot get over an election that was two years ago? I know many conservative friends who were willing to give Obama a sporting chance even though they didn't vote for him. When he turned out to be exactly what we had expected, we just went on with our lives and jobs. We were definitely more depressed when Obama was reelected. But I do not know a single person who would have considered for a minute barging into a restaurant and sticking appendages into the food of any elected official or Obama administration figure.

Well, to the salad-spoilers of America, let me give you a heads-up. I wouldn't try it in Arizona. I promise you I am not the only one who would take an assault on my salad as a life-threatening event and respond accordingly. I often chop my salads into tiny pieces with a meat cleaver I carry in an appendix holster when I'm out and about. Which would give new meaning to "Finger Food." Oh, and salad is one thing, but touch my dessert, and all bets are really off.

FAMILY THEMES AND GUIDING PRINCIPLES

November 2, 2018

It's been a tough week for us all and I felt it necessary to just step away from the vile, soul-sucking crap on the Internet. I offer this little non-political change of pace as a balm.

I was emailing Becki, a great new friend I met a year ago, and she mentioned that the motor force of her family, the Family Theme, if you will, was "What will people think?" I wish I had been imbued with more of that concern. Maybe that accounts for her magazine-worthy lovely home and pulled-together appearance.

Before I got household help, me, not so much. It's all well and good for a home to look "lived in," but probably not by goats.

But for better or worse, though my mother was a very kind, sensitive person (and, unlike her daughter, a world-class housekeeper), worrying about what "other people thought" was neither an overt nor unspoken value in our family. Mother was more concerned that one of us would "jump off a bridge if so-and-so did it." We were definitely encouraged to chart our own paths rather than blindly following the crowd in the bridge-jumping arena and elsewhere.

Mama's family was one of just three families in the tiny South Dakota town that wasn't Norwegian Lutheran, so they were oddballs right out of the chute. They were also rock-ribbed Republicans in the era of FDR and she swore to her dying day that beautiful government commodities – huge juicy oranges and grapefruits – were given to Democrats but not to them. It broke my heart to hear about it and, as adults, my siblings and I spent a small fortune sending her Florida citrus by the metric ton to try to make up for it.

Anyway, the discussion with Becki got me to thinking about our Family Themes growing up. For the life of me, I cannot come up with just ONE over-arching theme. I remember the classic scene in *Annie Hall* when Annie tells the Woody character that in her super-WASP Wisconsin family the biggest sin was "being too loud." (clearly, I don't think Woody Allen understood a thing about Wisconsinites...) But he replied that the biggest sin in his New York Jewish family was "buying retail." (For my Depression-scarred mother, the sin was more buying anything at all. "Make do." Boy, I hated those two words in that order!)

I was told several things repeatedly besides the universal "We'll see." (translation: "The answer is really NO, but I don't want to hear any more about it right now.") We were definitely not raised as Snowflakes. Neither parent could abide whining or tattling. We were raised to be tough. My tiny mother was the catcher on her women's softball team and could break an apple in half with her bare hands. "Stop crying or I'll give you something to cry about" was a frequent, though never carried out, threat from Daddy.

As conservative and somewhat retrograde as Papa could be, he had zero tolerance for weaseling out of difficult things because we were girls. I know it is not a universal experience for women of my era (The Pleistocene Age), but I was never told in any way that there was something I could not do or achieve because I was a female.

My maternal Grandmother, born in the blizzard of 1888, the ninth child in the family, was the one exception. She hated to see "young ladies" in pants, so when we visited, I had to wear a dress and sit quietly and – I am not making this up – embroider pillow cases rather than run around like a banshee outside. I loved her because she was my mother's mother, the visits were always brief, and it would not have surprised me to learn that she was really born in 1688. I thought she was well over 200 years old when I was 6. Of course, in reality, she was far younger than I am now.

But you know what? It never hurt me a bit to have to do something just because an older adult thought it proper. Respect. Not much in evidence today when a young cowardly thug can harass a 9/11 widow and wish her late husband to be burning in hell. My other Grandma, a Gold Star Mother, would have sent me there with a rolling pin had such a thought ever entered my mind.

I read once that a common saying in Japan is "The nail that sticks up is the one that gets pounded down." I lay no claim to expertise on Japanese culture, but it would seem to be an obedient and conformist culture. The type that our betters in the elitist class want for all of us unruly Deplorable-Americans, as long as what we're conforming to is their version of funhouse mirror reality.

That Japanese saying is as far from the American individualist spirit as it can possibly get. I was always jealous that "Live Free Or Die" as a state motto was already taken by New Hampshire. "Land of 10,000 Lakes" – THAT'S what you came up with instead, Minnesota? Inspiring!

Of all the crap that Obama delivered from on high unto us bitter clingers, perhaps the most ludicrous was his constant pronouncement that whatever we wanted – Voter I.D., secure borders, lower taxes, race-blind admissions – was "not who we are." To which I always wanted to scream, "How would YOU know who WE are? You spent all your formative years either eating Curried Dog in a madrassa in Indonesia, or smokin' dope in private school on an island paradise. Your experience as an 'American' carries exactly the same weight as Lizzie Warren's experience as a Cherokee. Like Sgt. Schultz, you know nothing! You can't even throw a baseball!"

But back to the themes and mantras in my family. These loomed large: Be kind. Be independent. Be brave. Do the right thing even when nobody else will. Do the right thing even when nobody else is looking. God is looking.

My Lessons in Economics: Never go into debt. If you can't save up for it, you probably don't need it. Whatever you want to do, we can't afford it.

On romance and homemaking: Don't put bananas in the refrigerator. And the boy won't buy the cow if he gets the milk for free.

From this sage advice — all well-intended, some ignored — and a ton of love, I made a life. How about you?

BOOK ONE ROLLOUT!!

November 9, 2018

Well, dear readers, this is IT! Remember that great scene in *The Jerk* with Steve Martin when his nebbish character, Navin R. Johnson, goes crazy with joy because the new phone books had arrived and his name was in them? Well, I am almost as excited!

Ammo Grrrll Hits the Target is out on Amazon. It is the compilation of columns from the first "Ammo Grrrll Year" which runs from the end of March 2014 to the end of March 2015. Attractively priced at $9.99 for the e-book and $15.99 for the paperback – well, it's attractive to ME, anyway.

A few weeks ago I also alerted readers to the opportunity to get acquainted with new writer, Max Cossack, whom I have seen shower. Just sayin'. Eat your heart out, Harvey Weinstein. I want to thank Power Line readers and friends who ordered Max's book ***Khaybar, Minnesota***, and especially those who were kind enough to review it favorably on Amazon. For those who have not yet bought the book, or who have bought it but not yet reviewed it, those opportunities still exist. Supposedly, the Magic # for 5 Star reviews is 50. Almost there!

But enough about Max. He doesn't even help with the dishes much. Write, write, write, write, write, that's all Max wants to do – several plays, many CDs full of music, and now, novels! He is hard at work on his second novel. Back to me!

Ammo Grrrll Hits the Target features all but a couple of columns from that first year, plus additional never-before-seen material and a very special surprise at the end. I'm not going to tell you what that surprise is, because then it won't be a surprise, will it? I am notoriously terrible at keeping secrets. Espionage would not be a wise choice of profession for me or anyone in my family. Here is an example of the secret-keeping chops in my family in a series of phone conversations, all within 10 minutes:

My brother Jim: How's everything?
Me: Good, how about you?
Jim: Oh, I quit my job, but don't tell Mom. I'm sure I'll get another one soon.
Me: It's a good idea to HAVE a job lined up BEFORE you quit, but whatever. I know you were unhappy there.

Phone rings. It's Mom.

Mom: Have you heard from Jim lately? I just have a bad feeling that something is wrong.
Me: He's fine. He'll be much happier now.
Mom: Now? Why now?
Me: (DOH!) No special reason. Okay, okay, uh, he quit his job. But, he told me not to tell you. So, for Pete's sake, don't tell him I told you, OK? Do NOT tell him I told you!

Phone rings.

Jim: What in the hell is the matter with you? I asked you not to tell Mom!
Me: I know. I'm sorry, she tricked me somehow. I specifically TOLD her not to tell you that I had told her!

See what I mean? I'm not good at keeping secrets, and I'm even worse at plugging my own work. Colonel Kurt Schlichter, a columnist I much admire, relentlessly pumps his books in every single column. That is his right and apparently okay with Townhall, but I tend to skip right over the plugs now. To avoid becoming a tedious pest, or worse, being fired, I promise to mention my book only every so often. Like if sales lag. Of course, I have no control over beloved readers, should any of THEM mention it every now and again.

However, you can do your part to keep the column commercial free by just ordering more books every so often and in mass quantities. For those of you who still maintain Facebook pages, maybe plug it there for me. For those without a Facebook account, you might consider sending out an email blast to everyone you've ever known who might still remember you, like I did. It also makes a fine gift for Thanksgiving, Christmas, Chanukah, Super Bowl Sunday, or Arbor Day. A personally autographed book LOOKS more expensive than it is!

There will be three more volumes in the series before I am current, one released every couple of months, and then one a year after that, God willing. As long as Power Line will have me. Thank you in advance for reading me and being more supportive than any writer has the right to expect.

If this book is not successful, I may be forced to be photographed naked. Apparently, judging by recent election efforts, certain unhinged women think this is an effective form of persuasion. Or threat. It wasn't exactly clear which. Let's just not let it come to that, okay? My book is only 6 x 9 inches. If that is all I have to cover myself with, I will be forced to make some difficult and disturbing choices.

By now most of what could be said about the election has already been said. I have just a couple of thoughts to add: Money alone was not decisive, as evidenced by the obscene amount squandered on "Beto," the Irish pretend Hispanic. Also, celebrity endorsements had little or no effect. Poor Babs Streisand will continue to get fatter from TDS and Ms. Swift opted to lose fans to no avail. Nobody gives a rat's patootie what Cher has to say and never will. It was a blue wave in a toddler's wading pool. On to 2020.

The important thing is my guy, Glenn Morrison, won for Constable. That and my book is out.

WHAT DO THE NAKED LADIES SAY?

November 16, 2018

I know whenever I wonder what side of an issue to come down on, the first place I go for guidance is to naked people.

Well, okay, full disclosure (as opposed to full dis-clothes-ure), I am but a poor clueless married white woman leeching off my husband, so the FIRST place I go is to ask my husband to tell me what I think. Hillary said so and, since even a blind pig finds an acorn once in a while, she must have accidentally got something right. Everybody who knows me knows I always seek my husband's permission before opining on anything, even the weather. But, after THAT, or in case he is writing, or having a nap, I seek out naked women for advice.

I have lived long and prospered in this great and good land. I am a reasonably intelligent person. And I cannot for the life of me figure out why taking off all your clothes strikes some women as a powerful tool for persuasion. Men, maybe, can be at least temporarily distracted by it, but why would it impress other women? I HAVE those parts, ladies. They are available for viewing every morning after my bath, and I must confess that there are times when I affirmatively choose NOT to look too closely, but sprint right out of the master bath in a large beach towel to a bedroom lit with only flattering candlelight to don something black or with vertical stripes. Perhaps if I "sprinted" more often these measures would not be necessary. But back to the ladies posing for naked election ads.

Possibly these are women who have for too long hung around icky men like Harvey Weinstein and Matt Lauer who consider naked subservience to be but the first step in any negotiation? Possibly a few of these more attractive women have found that getting naked helped them get a "leg up" in the business or entertainment world, or possibly even both legs. After all, Chelsea Handler's autobiography is entitled *My Horizontal Life*. Nuff said. So though I didn't click on her naked image, maybe she was really just showing off or advertising.

I remember several marches against various wars by the screeching harpies of Code Pink who went at least topless, if not stark nekkid, to draw attention to their cause. Because nothing says "War is hell" like wrinkled cleavage. Remember, young people: That tasteful little rose tattoo at the TOP of your breast can, in later years, become a long-stemmed rose down by your waist. Think before you ink.

Sadly, many of the Code Pink marchers, and many women in the naked midterm election picture undoubtedly stimulated in the viewing public, not political agreement, but immediate commitment to drastic low-carb dieting. If not deliberate blinding with whatever implements came to hand.

But I'm still trying to get a handle on WHY they thought it would be effective. What is the connection between nudity and political persuasion in their tiny minds? Now I'm going to say right here that I would mud-wrestle Nancy Pelosi naked in Macy's window if she were forced to convince the Democrats to fund and build the wall if she lost. But I can say that with complete confidence because it's never going to happen. And would, in any event, be a very unfair fight, even without involving firearms. My brother was a high school wrestler and I know some cunning moves. Plus, Nan looks like she would cry if you even messed up her hair.

I saw Chelsea in a little piece on Breitbart looking very haggard and the worse for wear after the election and she was just soooo sad and ashamed to be white. She had just learned that a sizable majority of white women voted for Ted Cruz instead of Dreamy Beto, the Drunk Hit and Run Guy. Oh, the humanity! And she felt very strongly that white women should NOT vote in their own self-interest but think of OTHERS. Haha, what a moron! Virtually every conservative position that is good for ME is good for everyone. The robust economy? Record employment? Respect for cops and the law? Stemming the tide of cheap, illegal labor? Which of these things is bad for people of color, O Bimbo in the Buff? Please describe and show your work.

All these pathetic losers can do is name-call with "sexist" and "raaacist" being two of the few words they know. Plus, "white privilege." Not even to mention that white women went for Cruz at about 59% whereas black women went for Beto at 95%! A great big ol' monolithic voting bloc, a "blacklash" as Van Jones would have it, but that's just peachy keen. However, if the white women vote splits 60/40, it's a sign of virulent racism! Never mind that "Beto" is as white as the driven snow and Cruz is not. Logic is clearly not the strong suit of a woman in her birthday suit. So just to be clear, 95 percent of black women voted for the white Irishman. What the heck? Do black women "hate brown people" which is the scurrilous charge repeatedly hurled at us citizens in favor of enforcing borders?

But back to the nudity. How come it's only women who get naked for a cause? You just never hear men saying, "We're going to take off all our clothes to promote the idea that we should lower the deficit." You may hear of men appearing in semi-tasteful beefcake poses for a calendar to be sold for a good cause. But my guess is that most of the buyers are friends, family and gay men. Women just don't have the same interest in random naked men that men seem to have in random naked women. Probably something to do with biology. Oh no, wait, I forgot that men and women are EXACTLY THE SAME, biologically. So that must not be it.

Now, fellas, I have seen some of you shirtless at ball games with sports team names spelled out across your chests, and Chippendale dancers most of you will never be. And that's okay, because nobody is breaking down my door begging me to dance around a pole, either. But, while I appreciate naked enthusiasm for sports teams, I cannot imagine modifying my political stances because of the sight of you. All due respect. So, I think nudity in the cause of politics is misguided at best, and dishonest at worst. Because, what is it really? Just a pathetic, sad cry for attention. Am I wrong?

Oh, and speaking of naked promotion, it has come to my attention that some of you have failed to get your book reports in in a timely fashion. I refer, of course, to your 5-Star Reviews of my book (and Max Cossack's) on Amazon. Tucker Carlson is #1 in Political Humor books, people, with 816 reviews at last glance; whereas, I am #32 in that category, with NINE reviews. Heck, even Max has 40 reviews, just 10 shy of the Magic 50 Number that Amazon prizes. See the difference? Only you can turn that around. Wouldn't it be awesome if a book with Power Line in the title was in the top 10?

BRAVE NEW WORLD

November 23, 2018

Well, L'il Jimmy Accost-Her has prevailed in litigating his inalienable right to wrestle young women for the mic. (Geez, isn't that pathetically phallic?) The Democrats did NOT prevail in stealing elections in Florida or Georgia. And that's all the politics I can stand today. In happy news, my book is selling well. Click on the cute little book picture on the book shelf below and get yours before Amazon runs out! Okay, I just made that up to encourage you to hurry, because they print the books one at a time as ordered. They are a dollar off for Black Friday and beyond!

But the big happy news this week is that our son sent us (by actual snail mail!) the school picture of our 13-year-old step-grandson. He is a very handsome young man, though I'm sure no more handsome than your grandchildren, if your grandchildren could be movie stars.

The sweet, round, dimpled 11-year-old face smiling at me from the fridge has lost its baby fat and has now taken on the contours that will serve him well in adulthood. Among his striking features, we noticed his perfect skin.

Our son texted us that he has "normal" teenage skin, but that there is now an option in school pictures: One can pay extra for some amount of airbrushing! What an extraordinary new world! It sounds like just one more pampered thing, but, actually, I approve. Thirteen (also 14-45) is a traumatic enough time. If some minor little thing can be "fixed", why not do it?

Now, speaking for myself, this would have resulted in no improvement at all to my senior picture, the only year for which we had pictures when I was growing up. I was blessed with clear teenage skin, praise the Lord, but a very prominent nose. So, my picture would have needed a virtual nose job rather than airbrushing. And a much better hairdo. Maybe a makeover. And a more flattering outfit. Other than that, it was just fine.

The only time I ever had a skin "eruption" was on Prom Night when a zit appeared – of course, it did – right on my nose. Yes, the feature that I most wanted to draw attention away from, sprouted a great big ugly red glowing welt, such that, like Rudolph, I could have guided Santa's sleigh with it. Seriously, Lord? THIS was a critical part of your grand eternal plan?

If suffering builds character, I must have character up the wazoo. "Character" must be the only thing that a teenage girl prizes more than "a good personality" in that famous fix-up line: "No, really, you'll like Susan. She's not fat and she is pretty funny and she has a great personality … for a manic-depressive…mostly manic, actually. Did I say funny?"

How we get through high school still ambulatory and not permanently in the fetal position is anyone's guess. Two groups of people seemed to have fared the best back in my day: good-looking girls and athletic boys. The adult men I have known who were star athletes in high school retained a high level of confidence throughout their whole lives.

Randy, one of my best friends back in Minnesota, was a track star in a large high school in Iowa. He set records that endured for over 25 years. He ran track competitively for the Army before he got sent to Vietnam. From being a top athlete, he came away as one of the three or four most self-confident people I have ever known. From surviving Vietnam, he came away fearing nothing ever again. But, Lord, at what a price.

The Paranoid Texan Next Door was captain of everything – football, basketball, track. He is modest as well as paranoid, and pooh poohs the whole thing by explaining that the school in his Texas town was so small that everybody had to be in everything in order to field teams. But I believe those athletic achievements helped give him the confidence to go from college into Information Technology (IT), for which he wasn't formally trained at all. The whole field was in its infancy. What probably helped even more was that he was also valedictorian. Yeah, come to think of it, I bet that was decisive.

Being a really beautiful girl is more of a mixed bag in my observation, from knowing a few. On the one hand, it would seem to be a sure-fire ticket to wealth, fame, and happiness. The "average" among us might wish for a chance to find out. But life is more complicated than that. Several gorgeous actresses, most notably, Elizabeth Taylor, Delta Burke, and Kirstie Alley – really struggled with their weight. And were made the butt of cruel jokes when they failed at that. What wretched impulse is there within us all at one time or another that just delights in seeing the high and mighty laid low?

For even the pretty women that don't get heavy, there's no way – outside of dying young like Marilyn – to not get old. All the cosmetic surgery, Estee Lauder, Pilates, and dieting in the world will not stave off the inevitable. Women born in exactly my year include Dolly Parton, Susan Sarandon, Bette Midler and Cher. Dolly seems pretty centered, but I bet I'm the happiest of them all with my long-term marriage, modest lifestyle, fun careers as comic and columnist, and wonderful friends. (I take none of these blessings for granted, believe me.)

A whole new crop of lovely young ladies invades Hollywood every year. Women who were playing ingenues start to play the mothers of ingenues and then just disappear. At the

Oscars when they have the traditional tribute to stars who have passed away since the last Oscars, who among us has not said, "Holy Cow! I had no idea she was even still ALIVE."

The lovely Candace Bergen admitted in a sad interview decades ago that she searched the mirror every day for signs of aging. Some of the most beautiful women I have known are afraid that they are only prized for their pretty faces and that they are easily traded for newer models. Then again, I have also known a few who are pretty, smart, kind and psychologically healthy. Lucky ladies with lucky husbands.

To bring us back full circle to my opening thoughts about my grandson's airbrushed photo, if I could go back to that angst-filled time of life and change anything, I would not do it – even with perfect 20/20 hindsight – if it would mean that I would not end up exactly where I am today. On the other hand, if there is such a thing as reincarnation, maybe the next go-round, I could look like either Halle Berry or Grace Kelly. You know, just to see how that would work out. Pretty sure "Princess" would not be in the cards. I would be the worst one ever. Mr. AG – famous novelist Max Cossack – is cuter than Ranier anyway. Lucky me!

Have you ever seen a picture of Princess Grace in a Tactical Range t-shirt with holes in the bottom from bore cleaning fluid? I thought not. I bet she had staff to clean her guns.

SKOOL DAZE OR THE MORE THINGS CHANGE...

November 30, 2018

Columnist, historian, farmer, intellectual giant, Professor Victor Davis Hanson never fails to deliver a brilliant take on whatever he weighs in on. One of his outstanding traits as an essayist is his clarity. But, sometimes he lapses into Greek, Latin, Swahili or Sanskrit without providing a translation. I don't even think he is showing off; he seems like a very down-to-earth person. I think it's just normal for someone at his intellectual level. I find it sweet that he believes everyone is as smart as he is, even though, speaking strictly for myself, he is severely mistaken.

It does make me feel inadequate when I don't know what the foreign phrase means, like a few of Steve Hayward's The Week In Pictures offerings that I don't get but am too embarrassed to ask about. If I were in public, I would laugh anyway, like a kid who doesn't get the dirty joke but has to pretend to. Sadly, it is not yet illegal here in the United States to make someone feel "inadequate," but it probably will be soon. I just read an article that warned teachers in the UK – not at the kindergarten level, but at university! — to be careful in their teaching materials not to USE ALL CAPS, because it can frighten some of the students.

Oh, dear God. This, in a former empire on which, famously, the "sun never set." When Mr. AG visited The British Museum several decades ago and wandered about the incredible exhibits for days, he called me and said, "Apparently, if you conquer the entire world, you can get a lot of great souvenirs!" Mr. AG is a funny man.

So soon all that will be left of The British Museum will be the Exhibit of Unterrifying Lower Case Letters. And you thought there would never be a category weaker or more pusillanimous than "Snowflakes." Anyone scared of upper case letters is not even a snowflake, but a little melted puddle of yellow snow.

So, anyway, I do speak a "petite" amount of French, so I know that there is a phrase in French that goes *plus ça change, plus c'est la même chose*. Unlike VDH, I will translate: "The more things change, the more they remain the same." And ain't it the truth?

This was brought home to me most vividly one night in 1980 at 3:00 a.m., on my "lunch break" from my third shift job. A co-worker and I, who normally brown-bagged it, had left the typesetting plant and gone out to "dine" at Dunkin' Donuts in Minneapolis, to load up on sugar and caffeine to make it through one more night. It was located in a section of Minneapolis known as Uptown whose hipster residents had to show no fewer than 3 tattoos and 6 piercings to live there.

We sat in an uncomfortable plastic booth typical of fast food places where they want customers to move along briskly rather than lingering. Behind me I could hear the young singsong voices of two obvious teenage girls:

   "So, like, do you think he LIKES me, you know, as a friend or does he 'like, like' me as a girlfriend?"
   "I don't know, did he talk to you at your locker?"
   "He said, 'hi'."
   "Did he said "hi" with your name or not with your name?"
   "He said, 'Hi, Vanessa.' I'm pretty sure."
   "So, like, he knows your name then."

"Well, yeah, he's in my Remedial Algebra class and was also, like, in Summer School, I think, but, like, we didn't go that often. Like, I have to go again this summer."

Suddenly I was transported back to about 1962. It reminded me of a hundred conversations with my two besties in their basement, parsing the nuances of extremely abbreviated conversations with boys we fancied who were blissfully unaware of our existence. We were looking for the most minute clues and indications of any slight interest in us. We all should have become Forensic Detectives. Without advanced voice detection equipment or any of the modern wonders, we tried to figure out whether smiling and just saying "Hi" indicated greater interest than not smiling but saying, "Hi, Susan."

Oh, God. I wouldn't go back to high school for a billion trillion dollars. Although, I guess with that kind of walkin' around money, I could just BRIBE boys to talk to me.

"Hi, Barry, would you like to go to a movie and get a burger? You can drive my Corvette, and keep it afterwards. I'll buy the burger. With fries. Would you by chance be interested in owning Osterberg's restaurant? Cuz I could make that happen."

I am now closing in on my point. Back at the Dunkin' Donuts, my curiosity finally got the best of me and I turned around to sneak a peek at the young ladies behind me. I half expected to see girls in bobby sox and pleated skirts, white blouses with circle pins on the Peter Pan collar, saddle shoes or penny loafers.

But no. There were two young women with stark white makeup, black lined eyes, multiple piercings – eyebrows with safety pins, noses with rings, about 20 holes in each ear — all black raggedy clothing and blood red or white lipstick, what at least at the time was known as "Goths." A comedian friend of mine, Dean Johnson, used to have a bit in his act where he described the Goths who lived in his building and then asked, "What do they do for Hallowe'en? Go out as investment bankers?"

There they were in all their Nihilistic Chic glory, trying so hard to make some kind of statement, but all they really wanted was someone to love them. Just like when we were teenagers. "The fundamental things apply as Time goes by."

There are supposed to be 57 genders, give or take, which, theoretically, should double or quadruple the odds of finding SOMEONE to pay attention to us and love us, right? But transgender men trying their best to be "women" are still upset and disappointed that actual men do not want to date them. You just want to shake the person – not in a harsh way – and kind of scream – not in a cruel way – "WHAT THE HELL DID YOU THINK WAS GOING TO HAPPEN??" (Forgive the scary caps. I'm yelling. I admit it.)

My two little Goths in Uptown Minneapolis would be well into their 50s by now. I hope they found someone not just to LIKE them but to "like, like" them. Maybe even love. There's nothing like it in the world. It changes everything.

REPULSI-CANS

December 7, 2018

I really want to know where I can go to get a gig as a pretend Democrat attacking other Democrats on television? Would that be a dream job, or what?

There was chipmunk-cheeked Ana Navarro, on election night 2016, who was terribly excited about the pending, in-the-bag defeat of Donald J. Trump, as "sweet sweet justice" when Hispanics would get to deal him the mortal blow. Not being one who ever watches televised Pravda-like news, silly me, I didn't even know who the heck she was. Or, more accurately, who the "hack" she was.

And imagine my surprise, then, to see the chyron under her name describing her as not only the Professionally Hispanic Diversity Drone on the panel, but also a REPUBLICAN. Who wanted the Republican candidate for President to be defeated! Say what?

And just a few weeks ago, our Ana announced that she would vote for Gillum because DeSantis was nothing but a Trump "mini-me." Ooooh, good one, Ana. Tough noogies, o fake Republican — DeSantis won. Eventually.

Ah, I am so old that Chet Huntley and David Brinkley – on the only network we got in Alexandria when I was growing up – read the news in a sober fashion and, reputedly, one was a Republican and one a Democrat, and we never had any idea which was which, because…wait for it…they were actual JOURNALISTS. Remember when that was a thing? They had gone to schools in which they were taught to be "objective" and "unbiased" and "neutral" to the best of their ability. Isn't that a quaint and hilarious notion?

But anyway sometimes on those old-timey news shows there would be a panel with a Democrat who would express opinions on behalf of the Democrat Party and there would always also be a Republican who would represent the views of the Republican Party in a collegial and civil fashion. If there was ever a Republican featured whose sole purpose was to ATTACK other Republicans, I must have missed it.

So this is a whole new page in the Pravda playbook. It involves employing aging hacks like another pretend Republican and former Israel supporter, Jennifer Rubin. You know, old Karl Marx got most things wrong in his disastrous tome, but one thing is true: there is a "logic" involved in taking political positions. Little Jenny can start out abhorring DJT's "tone" and, if Orange Man Bad is her sole motivation for everything, and Orange Man is a staunch supporter of Israel, she can end up in the same camp as vicious anti-Semites and anti-Israel activists.

And a whole lot of other Never Trumpers can end up in that same boat, cruise ship, whatever.

The news shows must think that having a pretend Republican attack Republicans really impresses the average Republican. I can't speak for all conservatives, certainly, but to me, the very idea is REPULSIVE, not impressive. I hold Loyalty – to family, friends, country – to be an important virtue. I don't think most people of integrity much prize loud-mouthed turncoats. Collecting their 30 pieces of silver to talk trash about former allies. Especially in what is clearly a winner-take-all cultural war.

It's one thing to just be honest and upfront. When I realized that the Democrat Party – for which I had voted for over 30 years – had morphed into something unrecognizable and unsupportable in the areas of abortion, immigration, attitude toward Israel, and First and Second Amendment rights, I did not try to monetize my disgust by continuing to pretend I was a Democrat while loudly and viciously attacking every single plank of the Party. No. I just concluded: "I guess I am no longer a Democrat. So I must be a Republican. Holy Cow! Mom and Dad will be so pleased." And then I registered Republican and got on with my life.

Mr. AG and I both lost work because of it and a few – not many – friends. One friend, a great guy who thought he was being amusing, remained friends but introduced us at dinner parties as "These guys are Republicans, but they are NICE Republicans." Uh, okay, not like those other troglodytes. Cute.

Ms. Navarro, Ms. Rubin, and a raft of Never Trumpers should face the mirror one day and intone, "Well Hell's bells, I've turned into a gun-grabbing, border-erasing, cheap labor-loving globalist, terrified of the climate. I must now be a Democrat!"

But evidently, there's not much money in that since all the good official Democrat hack gigs are already either taken by entrenched Democrat hacks or not available to anyone who can't check at least two Professional Victim Boxes. Where's a nouveau hack to go to find work?

Since I don't watch television, I need people to tell me if any news outlet employs fake DEMOCRATS who attack the Democrats, or if this is just a Republican job opportunity. Occasionally, Alan Dershowitz disagrees with the Democrats on silly things like presumption of innocence or the right to confront one's accusers, and that takes courage. But, to my knowledge, he doesn't specifically attack the Democrat Party.

Which is a shame, and I think he should come over to the "dark side" where, as the joke t-shirt says, "we have cookies." But I kind of admire both his misguided loyalty to his Party and his integrity for departing from the Party line when it violates Constitutional rules of law or the norms of human decency. I think when the chips are down he will eventually be on our side. Ana definitely will not.

Ana and Jenny have the right to bloviate all they want about anything as long as they make no invidious comparisons about Valerie Jarrett's looks. But why they get to continue to claim to be Republican surely violates all "truth in advertising" standards.

I understand that there was some sort of petition asking for redress of this grievance, signed by many prominent actual Republicans. It apparently had no effect. So the Repulsi-cans blather on. Oh well, from the few times I have chanced to hear either woman yakking, I think we can safely say that their sphere of influence must be close to that of Kathy "Severed Head" Griffin, but well below that of Cher or Lena Dunham. Which is to say, nobody cares and probably either changes channels or puts the telly on "Mute."

WORST SONG EVER WRITTEN

December 14, 2018

It is time for another of my patented *Break From Politics* columns. Scott has graced us with beautiful and interesting musical offerings and commentary for many years, in an effort to preserve his – and our – sanity. Today, however, we will be talking about a very, very stupid song. And not even a recent one.

Everyone has a contender for the worst song ever written. Dave Barry used to ask for nominations in his periodic columns asking for readers' most hated songs. In 1992, the song I will discuss today "won" a Dave Barry reader poll for "Worst Lyrics" and "Worst Song of All Time."

Wow! It's a very high bar for worst song in my opinion, when you include everything from "Lollipop" to "Red Solo Cup" (which I like and Mr. AG hates, loathes, and detests. I can literally make him leave the house with it! Which comes in handy) and anything at all in rap.

I do not HATE the song we are about to discuss. It is catchy, musically complex, and reasonably pleasant as long as you don't actually listen to it. Because when you listen to the words, you realize that it is mind-numbingly stupid. Nevertheless, it sold millions of copies and has been covered by dozens, if not hundreds, of artists, including Richard Harris, Donna Summer and Waylon Jennings. Which goes to show you what I know. Mr. AG and I didn't think Madonna's coffee table book called *Sex* would sell either. Haha! We are a couple with our fingers on the pulse of the popular culture! Not.

Anyway, I won't keep you in suspense any longer. My nomination for worst song ever written is in agreement with

Dave Barry's readers: It is "MacArthur Park," particularly the version screamed by Richard Harris..

Not one word makes any sense, and I am cursed with an addiction to Logic. Jimmy Webb wrote it and, undoubtedly made a fortune off of it. He is a very successful songwriter with such hits as "By The Time I Get to Phoenix," "Galveston," and "Up, Up and Away." So, he can turn to me and say, "If you're so smart, why aren't you rich?" Point taken, Jimmy.

Still…Let us examine it, line by line, shall we?

Someone left the cake out in the rain.
I don't think that I can take it,
Cuz it took so long to bake it;
And I'll never have that recipe again.
Again.

"Someone left the cake out in the rain." Alrightie. It's not a picnic. There's no mention of fried chicken or potato salad. Just a cake.

Now, if you were outside, eating just cake, and a sudden squall came up out of nowhere, couldn't you have said, "Hey, somebody, grab the cake"? For that matter, since the cake is so all-fired important to you, why didn't YOU grab the cake instead of blaming this mysterious "someone"? (Remember, as Mama always said, "when we point a figure at someone else, three fingers are pointing back at us.")

But, okay, mistakes happen. The cake is out there. In the rain. And now, you don't think that you can TAKE it? Good Lord, man, get a grip. You're falling apart because of damp cake. And why?

Oh, because "it took so long to bake it." Well, in point of fact, almost all cakes take about 35-50 minutes to bake. If you bake it much longer than that, you don't have a cake, you have a doorstop. But, you're asking us to believe that because a cake that took well under an hour of your life to bake – during which time you can pretty much go about your business unimpeded – because this cake is ruined, you've lost the will to live?

And yet, you didn't grab it when it started to sprinkle! Curious.

No wait, here's another reason. "I'll never have that recipe again."

Oh, for Pete's sake, why not? THINK! Where did you GET the recipe? What did you DO with it? How long ago could it have been? Have you tried the Internet? And guess what, friends, the rest of the words make even less sense:

Spring was never waiting for us
Still it ran one step ahead
As we followed in the dance in the
Sweet green icing.

That, my friends, is not some kind of high-falutin' "poetry" too esoteric for us rubes to comprehend; it is gibberish. That's "fish in a barrel" territory, beneath even making fun of it.

Sorry, Jimmy, you've written some great things – but this is just embarrassing. It also does not work as a metaphor, as you claim, for the breakup of a love affair.

If the "cake" represents a love relationship and the relationship is floundering – "in the rain", if you prefer – follow my wise Mama's advice and "Come in out of the rain." Get some counseling, buy some flowers, apologize if you've been a jerk. I doubt the particular relationship "took so long to bake" because most celebrity relationships are measured in weeks and months, not years. And if the whole relationship "cake" got wet and fell apart, why would you want to use that same "recipe" again? Just reasonable questions if you're going to pretend it's all a grand metaphor.

Ah, well. Mr. Webb can just laugh all the way to the bank. It beats the heck out of the lovely and haunting rap ballad my foster son used to play, "The b*tch bettah have my money." What a beautiful sentiment – last dance at the Prom material. I'll take the moist cake one any day.

THE PLAYHOUSE

December 21, 2018

Sometime in 1924, my maternal grandfather came home from a neighbor's farm hauling what he called "a chicken coop for my three little chicks." When his three small daughters, who were 3, 4, and 6 came running outside, they found a beautiful little white playhouse, about 5 or 6 feet square, sturdily built from wood with a steeped shingled roof and latching front door. (Even full-grown, I could still stand up in it at its highest point, although that's really not saying much. Plus, I am jumping ahead in the story.)

My mother was the 3-year-old and she remembered that exciting day for all of her life. We were told a more detailed version of that story as a bedtime story for years. The little girls could not sleep that night and begged to sleep in the playhouse. Naturally, that lasted about 15 minutes until they heard a Hoot Owl and got scared and came back inside. But the playhouse remained their one toy – apart from a few dolls, a red wagon and a toy telephone – they had for their entire childhoods. And the Depression hadn't even hit yet.

People just didn't have all the STUFF we have now. (Go to your kitchen. Look around. I'll bet you a free lunch if you come to Arizona that you have enough dishes, stemware, utensils and cookware to outfit another one or two homes. Am I wrong? And that's just one room. Okay, now come back and finish the column.)

Children in Mama's day were kind of miniature adults. Even the smallest kids had farm chores – feeding the chickens, slopping the hogs. Mama said that what they mostly did in the playhouse was clean it. An uncle who was a prosperous carpenter in town gave them a doll buggy for someone's birthday. Mother would dress up the baby pigs in doll clothes and take them for rides in the buggy. She tried it with cats and chickens as well, but it didn't work out.

They were little girls, in training to be housewives and mothers. So they played with dollies, served endless tea, and took the few little furniture items out of the house and scrubbed the floor and put everything back. She said that they could send away for tiny samples of dry goods like baking powder, flour, and coffee, kind of a primitive version of Amazon. Sadly, there was no Internet to check to see that their package was "9 stops away" like now. They would trudge down the long driveway to the mailbox day after day to check and finally a little tin of tea or a miniature sack of flour would arrive!

My grandparents lost the farm, moved into one small town in South Dakota, got another farm when the economy improved, and, after Grandpa got Parkinson's, sold the farm and moved into a small town in Minnesota. The playhouse came with them in Grandma's back yard. By this time, of course, Mother and her next-older sister had married and produced six kids between them. The oldest sister, mildly handicapped from a difficult forceps delivery, never married. She doted on us nieces and nephews. We loved her dearly.

Visiting Grandma and playing with the cousins was a treat about three times a year. Well into my early teens, the playhouse was a source of fun. We played "House," of course, as smaller girls, but also "Alamo," "Emergency Room," "School," "Miss Kitty's Saloon" (complete with choreographed fistfights) and "Pirate Ship." It was best to play outside where Grandma couldn't see that I was wearing slacks and not sitting quietly in a dress embroidering dishtowels or pillowcases.

Is there any family untouched by tragedy? Our oldest cousin drowned in a terrible accident between his sophomore and junior year of college. The rest of us grew up and married and most had children of our own. Grandma moved into a nursing home and the playhouse went to my parents' home for my young son and my brother's kids to play in, the third generation of children to enjoy it.

Our son loved the playhouse. By this time the playhouse had been re-roofed and a few rotting boards replaced, but it had now been around for over half a century, in pretty brutal weather. It was now outfitted with relatively expensive toys, "wall-to-wall" carpeting, and more "boyish" toys like blocks, trucks, LEGO, and guns. Girls had dominated previous generations, but boys were not going to be entertained with dolls and dishes, no matter how "fluid" anyone imagines genders to be. They aren't. Take away little boys' guns and they will use a carrot or a banana as a gun. Or, God forbid, chew their Pop Tart or bologna into the shape of a gun.

The grandkids grew up, as grandkids will, and one granddaughter had kids. The FOURTH generation in the playhouse. But my parents were now in their 90s and moved into Assisted Living. The family home was eventually sold to a divorced lady with three little girls, like everything had come full circle. We were very happy about that and cleaned up and painted the playhouse for them. We bequeathed them a variety of Fisher Price and PlaySkool toys and fancy child-size furniture that went with the playhouse.

Alas, when I visited my parents in Assisted Living just a few months later, I made the mistake of driving by my childhood home. The new family had already got rid of the playhouse! It was like a punch in the gut. I did not tell my mother, but a neighbor did. Mother was sad but resigned. No member of our extended family had had room or use for it. At the time, only two grandkids out of five had children. One already had a modern plastic playhouse for her kids.

We lived in Arizona where getting it here "on spec" for a future grandchild would have cost a small fortune. We have rocks and cactus for a "yard." You don't tell a toddler to "go play in the cactus." Plus, the HOA busybodies would have had a conniption fit even if it had been painted one of the 8 approved colors. There comes a time in most families when there is nobody appropriate to pass a beloved heirloom on to.

It seemed to me it was kind of a metaphor for many things – the relentless march of time, the difference in expectations of a simple Depression-era child and a modern kid. Nothing lasts forever. Not even a sturdy playhouse built with love and good lumber in 1924. But, on a positive note, it was great fun while it lasted. I couldn't calculate the thousands of hours that little children had enjoyed it. And it had a helluva run, just shy of 90 years. Not bad for any piece of real estate before it becomes a teardown.

Today is the closest to Christmas that a once-a-week columnist can come. So I want to wish everybody a Very Merry Christmas. Next Friday will preview the impending release of the SECOND VOLUME of Ammo Grrrll columns called, *Ammo Grrrll Aims True*. It's pretty darn funny.

THROWN OFF THE GRID

December 28, 2018

If you have ever had the highly unpleasant experience of having your car towed — when 300 yards down the block there was a tiny paper sign in 6 pt. type informing people that cars would be towed after 4:00 p.m. — you know that for just a minute your upset brain thinks, "Ah, that is inconvenient. Now I must drive my car to get the car...oh, wait..." And it sinks in that the VERY THING you need to solve the problem of having no car, IS your car! Which is gone.

Likewise, I woke up a couple of weeks ago on a Thursday morning, got myself fully caffeinated, made the bed, and went whistling to my home office to fire up the computer and check to see if I had email from my beloved in Israel.

When I hit the little Email icon, an annoying box covered some of the screen and told me that I needed to confirm my User Name and Password. No worries. By a Christmas miracle, I remembered both and typed them in. Confidently, I hit "Send, Receive" again. And the box reappeared with the same snotty demand. Oh, boy. Not at all good. Swearing at it was shockingly ineffective.

It is remotely possible that somewhere in a Memory Care Unit in Uzbekistan there is an ancient woman with fewer computer skills than I have. Though, I'm sure her great granddaughter is a whiz. Add to this the fact that I have the patience of a wet cat and you have a person whose systolic blood pressure is soon far higher than her IQ. Possibly for many more days until "Max Cossack, the famous novelist" gets home.

Naturally, I needed to Email Max to tell him that my Email wasn't working, but that couldn't be done. He is also a very peripatetic traveler who wanders about at will without previous reservations, so I had no idea where he was except "Israel," which may not be a yuge place, but big enough. Why not call him, you ask?

Well, because he had told me that his cellphone, some sort of inferior model from Big Bob's Bargain Phone Emporium and Fill Dirt, was not holding a charge and he didn't want to use it unless it was plugged in to a charger. So, I couldn't really call him to have him help me out. Plus the 9 hour time change difference was also a complication.

Upwards of 200 times I tried to just hit "Send, Receive" FAST enough, before the box appeared, thinking I could eventually wear out its desire to thwart me. Surprisingly, this was even less effective than the swearing, and now my DIASTOLIC Blood Pressure was in three digits, which is never a good number of digits for that.

So Thursday was a dead loss for solving my problem. Calling Customer Service was likewise frustrating, as the disembodied voice kept telling me that they had never heard of me, my zip code or any of my phone numbers. I tried it in Spanish just for a change of pace. Nada. Plus, they were hanging up on me as you would on an annoying teenage prank caller. Being a mature adult, I did some meditation to calm down. Then I ate an Edwards Key Lime Pie and finished off half a bottle of coconut rum with a quart of Eggnog. Then I napped til Friday.

Friday dawned cold and clear and the problem remained, of course, but I saw that "Max Cossack," who, by the way, has a great novel available on Amazon, had commented on my column! Wahoo! Thank God I at least had Internet. Now, I had a way to communicate with him. I told him and all the world that I had no Email and received such helpful suggestions as "I am sorry I can't come help you" from an IT whiz in Boston and "Have you tried the Paranoid Texan?" from the PT's best friend's wife near Fort Worth.

Max tried gamely to do some things from his hotel somewhere in Israel, possibly Haifa or Tsfat, (also spelled Safed, because, why not?) and thought he had made some progress. But the box reappeared and I resigned myself to having no Email for weeks. Max was exhausted from a day of exciting tourist adventures and retired for the night. The last thing he told me was to go get the Paranoid Texan. Neighbors summon the PT like you would, say, Reacher.

I was fresh out of Biscuits and Gravy so, like the proverbial Little Drummer Boy, I started making my excellent Meat Loaf, so I would have something to offer him in exchange for his expertise, not that he wouldn't do it out of the kindness of his heart.

Max had told me to write down some stuff which I showed to the PT. He opened some windows and fiddled with things, which I would never dare do for fear of crashing the entire Internet. Or worse, deleting Max's new novel or my next three books of columns. The PT may be paranoid, but he is a definite Alpha Dog when it comes to computers. Not even remotely intimidated, he went into secret areas of the computer and clicked on a thing called "Repair." I hid in the kitchen, my Safe Space. He said, "Come back and try Email." I did. No box!

I hit "Send, Receive" and 282 emails popped up, all but 10 completely worthless unless I wanted to order grapefruit from Florida, look at swimsuits, or find out the specials at Elden's Grocery Store in Alexandria, Minnesota.

Periodically, people entertain fantasies about living "off the grid." Back in the day, it was popular for hippies to claim they were going to "live off the land." They quickly learned that farming and ranching were way too hard for the likes of spoiled, lazy, blissfully-ignorant Utopians who would have starved within weeks. The Paranoid Texan tapes and enjoys many shows about living off the grid for real in Alaska. It may have its charms, but it is a perilous and difficult life, not for sissies.

Other than shooting, I have not a single survival skill, unless you count whining, which is just as likely to get you killed as helped, and not without reason. Even before shoulder trouble and encroaching decrepitude, killing, skinning and butchering an 1800 lb. moose into steaks, chops, and roasts would not have been in my wheelhouse. I understand from these programs that one has to work really fast to keep other lazy-ass predators from just taking your prized late moose away from you, like a "Fundamental Transformation Democrat."

I would probably give up a moose to a grizzly pretty fast. But if Amazon snowmobiled on by with Harry and David Truffles, or Rosati's delivered a 4-Cheese Thin Crust Pizza, Gentle Ben the Redistribution Bear would have quite the fight on his hands. Best advice, Ben: play dead and you may live to filch a moose another day.

JANUARY, FEBRUARY, MARCH, 2019

The new year dawned bright and cold and alive, alive oh, with dozens of wacky candidates for President on the Democratic ticket, including one in mid-January who felt it was important to share with potential voters, a play by play video of his semi-annual professional teeth-cleaning. This, from a semi-grownup who came perilously-close to winning a Senate seat – in Texas. (Spoiler alert: don't worry about it – since this compilation of columns is being released, nearly a year after the original column was written, he's already gone.)

This final quarter is a target-rich environment for a political humor columnist. Except for the fact that an alien visitor to this planet would have to assume that the columnist was smoking or eating, or doing whatever it is one does with peyote. Alas, it is no drug-induced dream!

We plow on with a critical analysis of schoolboy fart references in high school yearbooks, that loomed large in the Kavanaugh Supreme Court nomination. And then a takedown of the Jussie Smollett disgrace – a little-known gay, black actor who totally manufactured a "hate crime" upon his person. His is a preposterous, yet all-too-common story and he has stuck to his narrative right up to and including the printing of this book.

As with all anniversary columns, we end with a celebration called "The Column Turns 5."

"I'LL TAKE 'THINGS THAT ARE DEAD' FOR $200, ALEX."

January 4, 2019

STARTING WITH MY BATTERY

So, last week we talked about my Email suddenly deciding it had never heard of me. Then, while trying to be part of the Podcast with The Big Boys, my connection failed. But wait, there's more! At the very time that last week's column appeared, I was offering to take my housekeeper's teenage son to choose the enchiladas for a late lunch. We both got belted in to my Hyundai in the garage. I depressed the brake and pushed the starter button. The brake would not really depress, which was unusual. Pushing the button caused every bell, whistle, and light in the dashboard to flash in an annoying, fruitless manner, but no sound emitted from the engine.

If there's one thing an ex-Minnesotan can recognize besides the nasal drone of a fellow Minnesota-speaker, it's the sound of a dead battery. Who knew that extreme heat is every bit as tough on a battery as extreme cold?

The PT jumped the car. Of course he had jumper cables in a neat little carry-all in his truck. The PT's garage is cleaner and better organized than most operating theaters in hospitals. And he owns EVERYTHING that could possibly be needed in an emergency – extension cords in 6 different lengths; all manner of irrigation doodads; a generator; a chain saw; a wide variety of ladders from a two-step to the one that inspired "Stairway to Heaven"; and a 100-lb anvil he inherited from his granddad. You never know when you might be called upon to shoe a horse, come the Zombie Apocalypse.

Eduardo reluctantly got out of the car, Lunchless in Copa, and went home with his mother. The PT followed me to AutoZone where the mechanic verified that my battery was not just "pining for the fjords" as the Monty Python sketch about the dead parrot implied, but that it had, indeed, "gone to its Maker," and was now a "late battery." He expressed some surprise that it had lasted for just over four years as its normal lifespan was two years. He sold me a more expensive one, supposedly good for five years.

It took well under 5 minutes to install the new one and I was on my merry way, considerably merrier than a few minutes earlier. I did reflect on how changed my circumstances were from the time we had the battery stolen from our '68 Mercury in 1976 – in January, in Minnesota – when we had mistakenly gone to a wretched movie at a multiplex with money we had probably found in the couch. That madcap outing cost us $50, which was a giant blow to our budget.

This battery cost $160, installed. I would have preferred to buy another pair of boots, but it was no real problem. Hey, I had probably sold that in books – *Ammo Grrrll Hits the Target*, in case you have forgotten — during that week, thank you contributors very much!

One of the worst things about being poor is that it is just so stressful and damnably inconvenient. Being "comfortable" is so much easier on the nervous system. Too bad so many of us have to reach late, late middle age before we achieve that level of comfort, but better late than never.

ANOTHER DEAD THING — COURTESY

Is this even a value in America anymore? I still hang with salt-of-the-earth people from the Old School. Several friends – despite my begging them not to – still compose handwritten thank-you notes for casual dinner parties to which they have also brought a hostess gift! Gentlemen of my acquaintance, including the famous novelist Max Cossack, still carry heavy items for the women in their lives and even open doors. In total fairness to gentlemen, it was not men who killed chivalry – it was women. If you've been screamed at and called sexist enough times for the small courtesies your Mama taught you – especially in the South – eventually you will cease and desist.

I remember my mother told me, "On a date allow the boy time to come around and open the car door for you, but, if he's already in the restaurant ordering, best to just get out and go in." Mama was nothing if not practical.

I hear horror stories of nobody RSVPing today even for big expensive weddings, and then showing up for the reception dinner costing $150/plate with several extra relatives.

People talk and text in movie theaters, which is Reason #22 why I never go anymore. Having ruined that experience, they have moved on to text and phone at funerals, symphonies, and in heavy traffic at 80 mph. (Time for one more repetition of my favorite bumper sticker: "Honk if you love Jesus. Text if you want to meet him.")

Teenagers wear ballcaps at the dinner table and flip-flops to the White House. People of all ages, but especially young people, have passionate relationships with their phones, while ignoring real people right in front of them.

Geezers have always resisted and complained about the incremental cultural changes that depart from mythical Good Old Days. I get that. My own maternal Grandma thought everything went to hell in a handbasket when women and girls started bobbing their hair and wearing pants. (Whatever a handbasket is, beside a receptacle for us Deplorables.)

And then, lo and behold, in her mid-80s, Grandma up and cut off her waist-long braid that she wound around her head, coronet-style, and secured with odd hairpins, and got an Old Lady Perm! Grams gone wild! She never wore pants, though. Dad's mother either.

Does any of that really matter? What if the absence of (un)common courtesy, what we used to call manners, is like Mayor Giuliani's broken-windows policing? If courtesy is "broken" or "dead," is the next logical rung on the long descent into entropy, spittle-flecked confrontations with professors, shouting down invited speakers, an elderly Oscar-winning actor shrieking "F Trump. F Trump" at an awards show, or a hideously unfunny "comedienne" calling a member of the First Family the C-word while another one carries a bloody severed head? And where, then, does it end? Countless times I have thought, "Well, this is really the worst," and Mr. AG has always said, "Nope. There IS no bottom."

I plan to let my hair grow and start wearing dresses again just in case Grandma knew something important. Hillary only wears pants-suits. Coincidence? You be the judge.

HERE COMES 2019!

January 11, 2019

I definitely recall mentioning that 2018 seemed weird because it was my house number in Maplewood, MN for nigh unto 40 years. I have no such association for 2019, although I expect it to be a doozy. God only knows how many useless egomaniacal retreads will queue up to challenge President Trump in the Republican primary and the Democrat field will look like a cattle-call audition for the host of a new game-show called *The Hating Game*.

Metaphor Alert: When I was a young bride, hundreds of dog-years ago, we had another young married couple as friends. The other wife, Kate, and I were both just learning to play Contract Bridge. Mr. AG was already an excellent player. His mother was a Life Master at Duplicate and a math genius who also spoke seven languages. We had a special tablecloth for rookies with the conventions written on it. "If you have 16 points, evenly distributed, with stoppers in all 4 suits, open with one No Trump," for example.

I caught on to the game pretty quickly and particularly enjoyed playing defense, but it always made me nervous to play the hand and I would do almost anything just to be the dummy. "Why in God's name did you support me in spades when you had three spades to the nine?" "Because I wanted you to play the hand."

But, wait! It may LOOK like we're going to go down in flames, but we had a secret strategy – "When in trouble, give the lead to Kate." If there was no way to get from your hand back to the dummy where you had a couple of critical tricks, you could be certain that Kate would play the one card in the entire deck that would guarantee that you could make the contract.

Why do I raise this, decades after those idle hours of marriage-destroying card games? Because I think that no matter how many human errors The President makes, that we can count on the Depraved Democrats to do whatever is the one thing that will irritate the electorate enough to re-elect DJT. Please, God.

I believe that Hillary Clinton was coasting to a sure victory before she decided to insult half the electorate with outrageous and tedious charges of bigotry. She will have the rest of her privileged life to think about that decision. She explained *What Happened* in her stupid book's preposterous laundry list of blame. She won the election for Trump, that's what happened.

If either that pathetic, ungracious loser, Romney, or John Kasich, who wouldn't even attend the 2016 Republican convention in his home state, tries to challenge President Trump in the primaries, he will be squashed like a bug. Jeff Flake, with the personality and charm of a wet dress shield, would have the same chance as Creepy Porn Lawyer.

But, more importantly, on the Democrat side, there will be a real WWF cage match a-brewin' from all the competing segments of their "oppressed" entitled constituencies. It is possible that fickle Rust Belt voters could abandon Trump for a Biden or even a Bernie, if those codgers aren't upstaged by a younger dork on a skateboard with a fake Hispanic nickname. But there is no way that another old white man will be at the top of the Democrat ticket. Not when the Democrat Party's main propaganda wings in the media and Hollywood have been peddling anti-male, anti-white bigotry for the better part of three decades. There will be tremendous pressure for a "person of color," probably a woman, to head the ticket.

Eventually, SOME woman will be President and the fight to be the "historic first" one should be a real beaut. Hillary will still be vying for that even if it's from an iron lung in a Memory Care Unit.

Elizabeth Warren has now thrown her tomahawk into that fight. She hasn't got a prayer either. Both of those women are elderly, unpleasant, radical howling harridans, without a scintilla of charm, wit, or grace. And also, of course, fish belly white. I would be a better candidate than either of them and I would be a TERRIBLE candidate. ("Know thyself!" said one of them Greek philosophers – Socrates, I think, or possibly Jimmy the Greek. I know my political deficiencies, beginning with a jeans and t-shirts wardrobe, the inability to walk in high heels, a face made for radio and a voice made for the printed word. Plus a pronounced tendency to just blurt out what I really think. There's more – fear of flying, a desire to not leave my cozy house, irrational hatred of pantyhose — but I'll just stop here. It's a short column.)

Sadly, the American electorate has the collective attention span of a teenager with A.D.D., and a poorly developed sense of gratitude. A working class fat with higher wages, lower taxes, full employment, and a robust stock market, can easily forget what was in store for them if Hillary "We're Gonna Kill Coal and Open the Borders" Clinton had won.

The class of what columnist Colonel Kurt Schlichter calls The Normals elected President Trump out of a sense of desperation. But if Normals have it really good for four years, people forget who made that happen. They are vulnerable to being persuaded by a relentless onslaught from media and entertainment: "Sure, you are working now and doing well, but what about free health care, free college, free everything and a top tax rate for The Evil Rich of 90%? Think how great THAT would be!"

"Free Crap" is always a dangerously-alluring promise. Plus, any politician – from Churchill to Bush, Sr., to a lightning rod like DJT – can wear out his welcome. Especially with the vicious daily lies and hourly character assaults on Trump, unprecedented in my experience of a lifetime of political engagement. It can't help but have an effect.

Which is why I count on the "give the lead to Kate" strategy to save us. Or more accurately, give the microphone to the potty-mouthed radical dingbats and hope there are enough sane adults left to notice. One concern, of course, is that – with beheading "jokes," and the "c" word, "gash", and, now the "mf" word already used up – they will have simply run out of naughty words and actions that would turn off Normals.

And then I remember the ancient wisdom of that great novelist Max Cossack, AKA Mr. AG: "There IS no bottom." The Democrats will not disappoint. Witness their brilliant "Wall" rebuttal.

Happy 2019 to one and all. Stay strong and brave and in fighting form.

GOOD ORAL HYGIENE AND OTHER GOOD NEWS

January 18, 2019

In an amazing coincidence, I was having MY teeth cleaned the same week as Beto O'Rourke! Dental Mania! I did not think to livestream the event for my tens of fans. My hygienist is Laura, not Diana, like Beto's. And I knew you'd want to know that. By the way, my actual real middle name is Marie, so in the future, I would like to be referred to as Ammo Maria Grrrll (or Ave Maria, if you prefer). Cool Hispanic nicknames all 'round! What the heck happened to the cardinal sin of "cultural appropriation"? I can't wear hoop earrings, but this fourth-generation Irish skateboarding man-child can be called "Beto"?

I am thinking of what other events I could livestream to show what a regular, ordinary, presidential timber sort of person I am. Even though, as I explained last week, I am not even a presidential twig, let alone timber.

I have a routine colonoscopy scheduled for 2055 – I schedule them every 50 years — so stay tuned. It will be tastefully filmed, I assure you. When I was a new mother in S.F. in the early '70s it was not uncommon for people to have colorful photos and even videos of their childbirth experiences. Now, that is swell for a PRIVATE FAMILY memento. As party fare, not so much. Was it just me who thought so?

They put me in mind of a wonderful quote I saw from a little girl's book report, "This book told me way more than I wanted to know about penguins."

Well, several of those photos showed me way more than I ever wanted to see of my friends' nether regions.

"Would you like to see the hour-long video?"

"Uh, no, really, those Polaroids were fine. Do you have any more bourbon? Or some smelling salts for my husband? Boy, look at the time! Honey, didn't you have to change the oil in the car? No, Sunbeam, you're right that we don't HAVE a car, but he is going to practice on our friend's car in case we ever get one in the future."

Had I even been inclined to film my baby's birth – which I was not – "would you like to see a Caesarean?" is probably a non-starter, even in Crazy Cali.

AND NOW, FOR SOME EVEN BETTER NEWS THAN BETO'S CLEAN TEETH!

Alrightie! Volume 2 compilation of Ammo Grrrll is out on Amazon. *Ammo Grrrll Aims True* covers the "Ammo Grrrll Year" from March of 2015 to March of 2016. It is a period fraught with drama, tension, unhinged celebrities, and more than enough Republican candidates to field a football team. With subs, coaches and equipment managers.

The 2016 campaign will also put the final nail in the coffin of pretend "unbiased" news. From here on in, there will be outright undisguised advocacy for the Democrats. Across the board. It had been ever thus for quite a long time, but the media had felt it was important to maintain a fig leaf of neutrality. Now there's no leaf or even a small fig to cover their perfidy.

Even Fox News got involved in the fun with snotty personal debate questions from Megyn Kelly. She disgraced herself, left Fox for greener pastures, in which, with breathtaking speed, she wore out her welcome with the folks she was sure would love her. She retired with only $69 million dollars, a Law Degree, and exceptional good looks to fall back on.

I wonder how unwelcome I would have to get to have the Power Line boys pony up $69 million to make me go away.

$69,000? How 'bout $69.00, fellas, which would finance a decent dinner out in the Dusty Little Village with drinks? No?

Well, then I guess I'll stay right here. I have only been alone with Scott once in a crowded restaurant. And other than once sharing a lane at a tactical range with John, well documented and with security cameras in abundance, I have never been around John without his stunning, smart, charming wife, Loree. I have never met Paul or Steve. So my chances of a #MeToo bogus lawsuit are slim and none, notwithstanding that in an embarrassingly large number of instances the accusation does not have to rise to anything more horrifying than a childish comment about a Coke can. So no big paydays for me.

Back to Book Two. I honestly believe that this volume will be a crowd-pleaser, containing, as it does, two of my very favorite columns, complete with pictures suitable for framing. Please buy the book, review it with 5 stars on Amazon, and tell your friends. Thank you. Your reviews for Volume 1 were beyond anything I could have in good conscience even made up myself. Mama, who thought I walked on water, would have blushed at some of the reviews. Bless you all.

My plan is to have Volume 3, *Ammo Grrrll Returns Fire*, out in mid-to-late-February. More or less. Give or take. Ballpark. That one will include my response to Hillary's bizarre and infuriating designation of you, me, and everyone we know as Deplorable. In a "basket," no less. And the actual election. You won't want to miss it. I hear it had quite the surprising outcome! But I don't want to spoil anything.

GIRLS (OF BOTH SEXES) GONE VILE!

January 25, 2019

As it happened, last week Mr. AG and a friend and I were watching a rerun of *Blue Bloods*, a series we quite enjoy. There was a scene set in one of those trendy, incredibly loud, incredibly crowded dance clubs that – to me – looks like the 10th Circle of Hell. (I think Dante missed one.) Then there was a VIP Room, an inner sanctum that the Really Kewl Kids aspire to, and outside that door stood a silent bouncer/guard who could have been the largest human any of the three of us had ever seen. He would dwarf Shaq. I kid you not.

He never had a single line of dialogue. Lord knows where they found him, probably in a real club. Mr. AG, himself over six feet, commented, "An ordinary man probably couldn't even reach his face with his fist." And Mr. AG has a reach like an orangutan. The script-writers never even pretended that anyone could fight him. He didn't have to say obscene things or carry a severed head to look badass; he just stood there calmly.

There is a pathetic trend in the last three years for short, muscle-free men to shoot their mouths off with escalating levels of obscenity. I speak of the late night Jimmy clones, interchangeable SNL cogs, the grotesque Mr. Colbert, and degenerate geezer actors like De Niro and Peter Fonda. In the Old West, these (Beta? Zeta?) males would find themselves unconscious on the saloon floor, if not on the losing end of a gunfight or duel. Andrew Jackson famously allowed himself to be shot first, took the round which was lodged near his heart till his last breath, and killed his adversary dead for impugning the reputation of his beloved wife. What might he have done to someone who called his daughter a "gash"?

I am not the first person to note that these Zeta Males, Democrats all, never fail to use anti-gay imagery in their insults. It's all perfectly kosher if you're a leftist. It started with actual gay man, Anderson Cooper, who saddled Tea Party activists with "Tea Bagger." Colbert referred to the President as providing a "c*ckholster" for Putin. I'd pay good money to fly Colbert to Russia and watch him say it to Putin in Russian.

As I write these words, there is a concerted attack once again implying that Senator Graham is gay and subject to blackmail. I neither know nor care whether Senator Graham is gay; he denies it, and after his masterful performance in the Kavanaugh hearings, I won't be criticizing him for many years, least of all for what he might do in his private life.

And what of the women? It is mortifying to me that most of these ranting harpies "identify as" comediennes. Except for the scrawny pitchman for potties shlepping the severed head, I can't even tell them apart. I've never heard a single one of them say anything FUNNY. Mean, yes. Nasty political commentary, at times. But not FUNNY. And always, always, obscene.

See, I KNOW funny. And I'm not a tough audience. Ask anyone who knows me, including my son. When someone would say something amusing and I would laugh my trademark cross between a shriek and a bray, often the person would say with some pride, "Wow, I made a professional comedian laugh!" And my son, if he was present, would say, "Mom laughs at everything!"

Neither is it just that I disagree with the women politically. I do, but it's not why I don't laugh. I found Jon Stewart quite amusing even when I disagreed with him. He had FUNNY things to say, with surprising punchlines, which is the essence of humor. I think Ellen is very funny. I have met her a couple different times and she is also a very nice person.

So what's up with all the "F" bombs and worse coming from the women "comics" and women politicians alike? They obviously believe they are demonstrating toughness with soap-worthy mouths and vicious attacks on their (approved) targets. They aren't tough. They are spoiled overpaid bullies. The second there is any sort of return fire, they either start bawling or run for the Race and Sex Cards in their fat purses.

Saying tasteless things as SNL's Sarah Beattie did, promising oral sex to any thug who would hit the MAGA-hatted Catholic teenager, is not tough when there are neither consequences for bartering for hired battery nor a means to compel performance of that promise. What would YOU do if she solicited battery against YOUR son? This crap has GOT to STOP. She needs to be prosecuted to the full extent of the law for solicitation of not just prostitution, but battery for hire. Criminal and civil cases. And fired from SNL. Enough! What are the chances in New York?

Enough with the fake tough girls. Tough is my paternal grandmother who bore six children and was a Gold Star Mother. Tough is Nikki Haley in the face of universal hatred from the General Assembly of the UN. Tough is Ayaan Hirsi Ali who risks her life every day and is "disinvited" by colleges as a speaker, for the sin of speaking truth to cowards.

Tough is Michelle Malkin who has to hire bodyguards for her threatened children. Tough is Sarah Sanders fielding hostile, repetitive "questions" (def: tedious bloviating speeches) from a gaggle of lacquered lackeys who have just received their talking points du jour from the DNC. Tough was my late friend Ruth, battling metastasized breast cancer for 13 years. I have broken into two all- or mostly-male professions, have stood on stage for an hour armed only with a microphone, and am pretty handy with a gun. Yet I am a pitiful CREAM PUFF next to the women I have named. And probably many women you know as well.

Caterwauling and scratching on the doors of the Supreme Court in silly little bonnets and *Handmaid's* costumes, pretending to be oppressed, does not make it so. Never in the history of the world have women had more opportunities or freedom than in 2019 America.

The humorless mean girls who think saying "MF" or "feckless c" is evidence of toughness are wrong. They aren't very bright and have confused vulgarity and bad manners with true grit. They risk absolutely nothing. The leftist cultural gatekeepers protect their own. It's going to be a long, potty-mouthed slog until November of 2020. Better invest in a good pair of earmuff ear protectors suitable for a construction site or the tactical range.

Mr. AG calls his ear protectors his "wife-suppressors." Now, THAT'S funny!

GEEZER FORENSICS

February 1, 2019

Sometimes, in the course of human events, your person of late, late middle age will sustain a strange injury which she has no idea how it occurred.

Let's say that, despite trying to limit her coffee intake to under 12 cups a day, for some unknown reason, she still has trouble making it through an entire night without getting up to use the bathroom. Let's further stipulate that she uses the time-honored "staying almost asleep" method of keeping her eyes shut on the way to the bathroom, during her time in the bathroom, and the return trip back to bed.

When she rams a hipbone into a bureau she may come close to opening her eyes and think, "Oh dear, that might leave a mark," but by morning that thought will have had no more staying power than the gauzy memory of a dream in which she is back in high school, inadequately clothed, of course, trying gamely to take a test in Calculus despite never having taken the class. "Cosine? Is that, like, when you stupidly agree to be a guarantor of your irresponsible foster son's apartment rent? Bad idea!"

In the dream, doing poorly on the test engenders much more anxiety than being in her underwear. And for some reason, the teenage boys around her are way less interested in her apparel than would seem realistic from her memories of those hormone-driven days. And no, it is NOT because she is her current age (late, late middle); in the dream she is once again a fetching teen herself. But, dreams aside, let's return to the trip to the bathroom and its aftermath. When an ugly bruise appears on her hipbone, she is quite mystified.

"Honey? Are you kicking me in your sleep? Or do you think it is from my seat belt? I probably shouldn't do the grocery shopping any more, or even ride in a car. I shouldn't even leave the recliner – unless the bruise is FROM the recliner…Maybe it is evidence of a nutritional deficiency and I am eating too few carbs. I bet that's it. Should I have another Mini-Muffin with my Mashed Potatoes and Gravy?"

Ah, but if that were the only injury, we wouldn't need the GFT – Geezer Forensics Team. When she next appears with a noticeable discoloration on her forehead and toothpaste stains on her t-shirt, the GFT springs into action and deduces from the spatter pattern of the water and toothpaste on her garment that what obviously happened is that she tried with wet hands and some difficulty to pull the brush-head unit off the motor unit of her electric toothbrush and, dislodging it at last, whacked herself in the head with her own fist in the follow-through. Ah, what was that thing about a body in motion tending to stay in motion? Damn, sexist physics!

Okay, that one wasn't an actual mystery. I was aware of what I had done at the time. [Abrupt change from third person to first person, because I feel like it.]

But, there was a real poser on my left arm: two scratches about two inches apart on the side of my wrist right below my hand and a sunburn-like redness on the wrist itself.

Mr. AG had not weighed in except to say, "It looks like nothing; let it go."

"But, but, but, how did it happen?"

"Who cares? Does it itch?" "No." "Does it hurt?" "Maybe a 1 on a scale of 1 to 10."

"A ONE? Good grief! Everything on my entire body hurts at least a 4 every morning when I get up."

"I'm not complaining, I just don't like a mystery." "You LOVE a mystery and read them all the time." "Yes, but that's because they are always SOLVED."

"Well go be mystified somewhere else. Don't you have some writing to do? Are there Lemon Bars in the freezer?"

Is this what we have to look forward to now? Collisions with sliding glass doors, falls, scrapes and bruises, a nasty tear from running into a cactus, and burns from teacups? TEACUPS, for Pete's sake! When my Primary Medical Consultant, Miguel the Produce Guy, quit his job at my supermarket, I was forced to rely on Woman's World Magazine for my medical advice. "Drink more tea!" they suggested, "You will lose weight and it's just chock-full of anti-oxidants." Not a mumblin' word about nuclear teacups in the microwave!

It occurs to me that being a senior is kind of like a Second Childhood only with more money. Remember Childhood when your limbs were a mass of scabs and scars, grass stains and floor burns? Here, a tumble down a hill on a piece of cardboard; there, a slide on bare knees across a wooden gym floor after the loose basketball; there, a collision in the dark with a barbed wire fence during Hide And Seek. And an impressive scar to show for it still.

We had no helmets for bike riding, no seat belts in the car. Parents didn't run to the ER at the drop of a hat. "Walk it off!" said Mama about my "sprained" ankle til Daddy came home from work and noticed the ankle was three times its normal size. Oopsie. Broken in two places, cast on from Memorial Day to Labor Day, fun summer. I learned to run the bases in the "walking" cast. Sadly, I wasn't even appreciably slower than before. Did I mention I had Poison Ivy on the leg when I broke it? Everything healed and we survived. Again.

That is what keeps me going – the knowledge that the human body is a truly miraculous healing machine. More slowly in late, late middle age, to be sure. But a miracle, nonetheless. Speaking of miracles, it appears that the Israelis may have cracked the code to cure cancer. Not a single country or government that supports BDS should get the benefit of it. Nor hateful anti-Semites in this country like the bigoted bigamist, Ms. Omar and her ilk. The Israelis would NEVER be that unforgiving, but I would. Hosanna in the Highest if this turns out to be accurate and not just another dashed hope.

Whatever was going on with my left wrist is almost better now. In the prophetic words of the late, great Emily Litella – God, remember when SNL was FUNNY??? – "Never mind."

YEARBOOK FORENSICS

February 8, 2019

Last week we had a lively discussion of Geezer Forensics, with many valuable contributions from commenters about their own encounters of the geezer kind with solid, unyielding pieces of furniture, sliding glass doors, boiling teacups, and the like.

Today, following the pathetic and ludicrous saga of Governor Coonhound (D) of Virginia, we will discuss Yearbook Forensics. Of course, by the time this runs on Friday, Dr. Bojangles the Baby Killer (D) may or may not have retired to spend more time with his family or work on his Moonwalk. Yearbook Forensics began with the Talmudic-level parsing of the Kavanaugh yearbook and has continued with the jaw-dropping photo in Governor Coonhound's (D) medical school yearbook. As everyone knows by now, there is a fetching Klansman next to a live lawn jockey. Sometimes you see something and your brain cannot absorb it ."Well, for sure that HAS to be Photo-Shopped!" you think. But, no.

Let's pretend for a nanosecond that neither idiot in the picture is the future Democrat Governor and Pro-Baby-Killing Pediatrician (Motto of his Pediatric Clinic: "If you don't kill your inconvenient clump of cells by the time it's been alive for 3 months, it's gonna need some DPT shots. We can help!"). WHAT in the name of all that's Holy, would have compelled a future doctor to think such a picture made a humorous addition to his personal page?

Let me be clear that I am not generally a fan of the "30 or 40 years ago this person said a naughty word or held a stupid political opinion" School of Inquisition. But, COME ON!! A Grand Kleagle AND a mortifying portrayal of a black person? SERIOUSLY???

In a typical high school yearbook, hormone-marinated youths delight in silly double entendres, braggadocio about their drinking and sexual exploits, at least 1% of which may have actually happened, and other childish nonsense. They are, after all, still technically children.

In my senior year high school yearbook, for example, several people have written "Take it easy on the boys this summer." Was little Ammo Student a hottie from whom the boys were in grave danger unless she chose to "take it easy" on them? Oh, if only. I certainly aspired to that, but it was not to be. When you have an average-looking, argumentative, bookish nerd who had to work six days a week in her Daddy's drugstore all summer long, it pretty much guarantees that the boys in her vicinity will be very safe indeed. At least for the summer.

Back to Yearbook Forensics. In case Hell does freeze over – what CAN'T Global Warming do?? – and the country decides it needs a "smart-ass" with no law degree, instead of a "wise Latina" as the next Supreme Court Justice, what would Spartacus, the Brilliant Drama Queen and Grand Inquisitor find in my yearbook?

To my horror, it actually LOOKS like there is a photo of me in blackface!

There was a "service club" in school, Sigma Beta Phi, called a service club because sororities were disallowed in Minnesota high school, and I had just been inducted. There was, of course, hazing. The new pledges had to go "uptown" in 1963 metropolitan Alexandria wearing bizarre costumes of the leaders' choosing. There I am, on the corner in my bathing suit, a grass skirt, and with the remains of a mud pack facial on my face (most had slid off). The mud pack was green, but it looks black in a black-and-white photo. It had absolutely nothing to do with race but try and convince a Twitter mob of that. Probably the grass skirt alone is enough of a cultural appropriation sin to sink my Supreme Court nomination.

I think I can kiss that lifetime job defending the Constitution goodbye. Crap. At least I have READ the Constitution and approve of it. Another point against me with the Democrats.

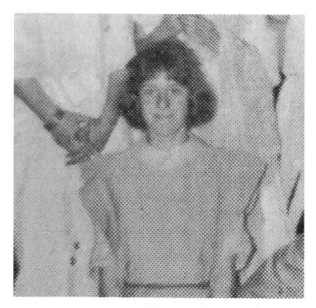

There is also a yearbook picture of me and several classmates in togas performing a little skit at the 9th grade Latin Banquet. My costume is a primitive rendition of a Roman centurion. Costume-making was never in Mama's wheelhouse.

At Hallowe'en she would just hand us all Bibles and send us out as Jehovah's Witnesses. I am so skinny in the Latin Banquet picture that it looks like some fatuous celebrity should organize a benefit to convince Ethiopians to send money to feed me. No eating disorder – I ate like a horse – just very ACTIVE. It is pretty striking in general that in the early 60s almost no teens were overweight. Out of 236 kids in my class, only 3 or 4 were overweight.

It appears that I wandered into several of the group pictures to give the impression that I was very active in extracurricular activities in order to pad my college applications. If I ever attended a meeting of either the Library Club, or French Club, I have no memory of it, but there I am. At least I read books and spoke French. It's a wonder I didn't try to wedge my way into the photo of the Audio-Visual Club, the wrestling team or the Homecoming Court in a Burger King tiara.

My best girlfriends wrote pages and pages of well intentioned, affectionate drivel in the yearbook, evidently in preparation for long-winded, tearful bridesmaids' speeches at wedding receptions. One did strike me: "Only those who have the patience to do simple things perfectly, will ever acquire the skill to do difficult things easily." Which explains a lot that has gone awry in my life, in retrospect. "Patience" at anything is not my long suit. Oh well.

I have amended that to "Those who have the patience to do unpleasant things adequately should be paid way above scale to do them FOR me. Failing that, find a husband who understands technology and – as a back-up — live next door to a guy who can do home handyman stuff." We have lucked out in both Minnesota and Arizona with finding that guy. Luckily, both of whom will work for food. Mine, at least.

Oh, I'll end with my most embarrassing yearbook moment. A girl I did not recognize, but who clearly appeared to know me, asked me to sign her yearbook. I threw a Hail Mary: "How do you spell your name again?" "A-n-n." "Oh, yeah, I figured that, but I thought it might have an "e" on the end." Pretty good recovery, eh? I have no idea who she was to this day, but I did encourage her to "take it easy on the boys this summer."

CHICAGO IS MAGA COUNTRY? WHO KNEW?

February 15, 2019

In the late '70s there was a horrendous spate of child murders in the Atlanta area. Once it became clear that a serial monster was on the loose, people sprang into action. It was all little black children, almost all boys. Racist slanders to the contrary, white people were just as appalled as black people. Committees were formed, ribbons were worn, buttons were sold that said, "Stop the Racist Murders." OBVIOUSLY, it was racist, right? Who in their right mind would believe that a black man had done such hideous things to black children? Then they arrested Wayne Williams for two murders and seemed to connect him to several others. He was black and the community reeled, so much so that there is still doubt that he was the one.

But save those "stop the racist attacks" ribbons because next came Tawana Brawley, pathetic little black girl attacked by WHITE COPS in New York who smeared her with dog feces. Again, white people were appalled, ashamed and even righteous cop-supporters were worried. What would make people do such a thing? Oopsie. She did it herself – with help – no cops; no white people. If YOU had participated in such a hoax, you might still be in prison. Ah, but not Al Sharpton. He has a job in television and owes several million dollars in back taxes. And you thought crime didn't pay!

Examples of other hate crime hoaxes of a racial nature abound, from "white" Hispanics to bananas in trees. Then just a few weeks ago, we got PROOF POSITIVE that a couple of white guys had walked right up to a car with a little black girl in it and fired bullets into the car without any regard for human life, killing the little black girl. Thank God we had EYE WITNESSES – the surviving family members of the murdered child told all and sundry that the murderers were not only white men but had blue eyes, that's how close they had been.

Oopsie. Nope. Just garden variety black thugs who may or may not have had a drug or gang beef with the "adults" in whose unfortunate care the little girl had found herself. We'll never know because there's nothing to see here anymore.

And now we have Jussie, gay black actor assaulted in Chicago. OMG, he says he went out for "something to eat" at 2:00 a.m. And that is the only thing he has said that I believe is true.

Let even the bare facts that we know sink in: he went out in absolutely frigid weather at 2:00 a.m. in dangerous Chicago. He couldn't have a pizza delivered? He couldn't make a peanut butter sandwich? The only people I have known who would go out at any time, in any weather, were hard-core smokers out of cigarettes. Or gay men looking for another anonymous, death-defying hookup. I have seen no evidence of a successful hook-up. But neither is there any evidence of a crime. So, how did the rope get around his neck?

Let's see – how to fan the flames of racist anti-white hate, get some publicity for his career, AND become some kind of martyr/hero to such morons as Cory Booker who thinks we need a new "anti-lynch" law. Because murder and assault are not already illegal. Not that Jussie was actually lynched, despite greeting the cops at his door with a rope still around his neck.

And who did this to him? Oh, but of course. Two white men who "recognized" him in a television drama not 12 white people in America probably watch, all bundled up in clothes in the dark so that probably his own mother couldn't have recognized him. My former gay, black hairdresser, now, sadly, dead of AIDS, said when he moved from the South to Minneapolis in winter, he thought he was the only black person in Minnesota because people were so bundled up at the bus stop that he couldn't even tell their race.

Jussie's racist attackers were just a couple of icky white people out at 2:00 a.m. carrying a bottle of bleach and a rope — on spec — just in CASE a random black or gay person happened to be out on the street looking for something to eat. Yes, happens all the time. Because Trump.

I know several dozen Trump voters personally. One thing stands out about all of us – the ones with the black or brown grandchildren, the ones with the gay children or friends, and especially those of us who are elderly and in bed by 9:00 p.m. – we don't always go out in urban America late at night. But when we do, we always carry noxious chemicals and rope so if we run across any of those "Others" Obama was always going on about, we can hurl appropriate epithets and bleach at them while saying, "This is MAGA country!"

But, wait, there's more! Ah yes, Jussie was on the phone with his manager at the exact moment when the attack took place! What ARE the chances? MY manager in Atlanta would have been just delighted to hear from me at 2:00 a.m. Did Jussie say, "Help, Mr. Manager, call 911 right now because some icky white people are attacking me?" No, probably not, but he won't give up his phone to the cops anyway. Did he take a picture of his assailants with that phone? No. Does he have any defensive wounds on his fists or DNA under his fingernails? We don't know. But, his manager DID "hear" the assailants yell, "This is MAGA country."

That is particularly hilarious. The two icky white MAGA people didn't STEAL his phone or dislodge it when they were putting the clothesline around his neck. They didn't even take his Subway. Uh-huh.

Let's say just for the sake of fun that the manager DID hear SOMEONE say, "This is MAGA country!" Jussie is an ACTOR. He can talk any way he wants to talk. Have you ever listened to a Book on Tape? ONE talented actor reads all the parts – men, women, Southern accents, black accents, old people voices – they can do it all. He says his preposterous story is "consistent." He is an actor. He memorizes a script every week.

But by all means, let's task the Chicago cops with looking through hundreds of hours of security tape in the area. Let's send them off looking for "Persons of Interest" all bundled up and also out on the deserted streets. It was well below freezing – where is the puddle of frozen bleach? Where are any blood stains from the alleged beat-down?

And what if everything Jussie said happened turns out to be true? Well, that would be a sickening criminal incident, not unlike what the elderly victims of the "Knock-out Game" must have experienced. Never heard of the Knock-out Game? There's a reason for that – the elderly white people who were smashed in the face were hit by young thugs of color as a kind of contest to see who could render an old white person unconscious with one punch.

Did Cory Booker or Nancy Pelosi ever weigh in on that, propose "anti-geezer beating" legislation, or send wishes for a speedy recovery to the victims? If not, then I have lost interest in their crocodile tears now. And those attacks actually happened.

MEDITATION ON GRATITUDE

February 22, 2019

Last Saturday, I read Scott Johnson's excellent column on the unseemly ingratitude of Ilhan Omar. Unfortunately, the day before, I had written an almost identical column to post this week. I sent mine to Scott with a laugh, accusing him of performing a Vulcan mind-meld, but he encouraged me to give it my own spin. So here is my take, with a bonus tacked on.

FIRST: MISERABLE PROFESSIONAL INGRATE

Try to imagine yourself being born a little girl in a war-torn land, run by lunatics and savages, each and every one the same color as you, the same religion as you, who enjoy removing critical parts of little girls' genitalia and dragging dead U.S. soldiers through the streets. Your homeland provides zero opportunity for you as a female person. If you live.

Now imagine that somehow you are part of the early wave of refugees who get to escape from this place President Trump correctly, if inelegantly, termed a "sh*thole." You get to go, say, to Sweden, where you are fed, housed, educated, given a free ride to college, and treated like a celebrity. Might you feel you owed the Universe one of the biggest karmic debts ever? What could you do to ever repay such generosity, such opportunity?

Might you grow up to be THE biggest cheerleader for your generous new homeland? Might you never cease thanking Allah or Jesus or Hashem or at least blind dumb luck for this great and generous country that plucked you out of certain disaster and set you up on a path to untold riches and fame? Well, no. Not exactly.

You will, for reasons that are completely unclear, hate everything about your new homeland and do everything in your power to recreate the very culture you fled. You will turn on the Swedes and try to ruin the society that coddled and protected you from your own kind.

But, of course, we aren't talking about Sweden or a random little refugee girl. We are talking about fraudster, bigamist, vicious anti-Semite, America-hater, and member of the House of Representatives, Ilhan Omar. She was not sheltered in Sweden; she was awarded THE Most Valuable Lottery Ticket in the World – the right to settle in the USA, sweet land of liberty and unlimited opportunity for everyone regardless of race, creed, or sex.

Unlike other earlier waves of refugees and immigrants, however, instead of being provided for by relatives or members of her wider community, she was supported by taxpayers and charitable givers who provided food, shelter, and education. Ah, but the largesse didn't stop there. In Minnesota, where Ms. Omar and up to 100,000 of her co-thinkers settled, there is a place called Neighborhood House, funded by generous contributors from several "faith traditions," but most notably Jewish synagogues.

Here you can take classes, learn English, study in a safe space if you are a student, pick up some free groceries, and line up for beautiful free school supplies for your children. I happen to know this because I have been a volunteer. I handed tablets, crayons, and backpacks to adorable little Mexicans, Hmong, and Somalis and the little Asian and Mexican youngsters always said thank you.

Never once did I get a thank you from the Somali kids or their parents. I only did it twice, so maybe I just got a particularly rude batch. Or maybe hostility, rudeness and entitled arrogance are either prized qualities in the culture or learned behavior once they get here? Watching Omar's rude KGB-like interrogation of Elliott Abrams confirmed to me that this woman displays ignorance and arrogance in equal proportions.

I am mortified for the voters in my home state of Minnesota who elected to send this bigot to the House of Representatives and for Nancy Pelosi who insisted Omar be placed on the Foreign Relations Committee where she could do the most treasonous damage. Shame. Shame. Shame. But at least Ms. Omar has chosen to focus on UN-Level Israel Hatred and the critical issue of men pretending to be women being able to compete in women's powerlifting. I will sleep well tonight knowing I do not have to worry about actual women winning that event ever again.

MOVING ON: PROFOUND GRATITUDE AND LEFTIST-ANNOYING JOY

In four short weeks, my column will turn FIVE. I cannot believe that I have been guest-blogging on this fine site for so long, and yet, I am only two years older! I'm pretty sure I look exactly the same, lying Driver's License photos notwithstanding. After the first couple of years, devoted commenters and readers clamored for a compilation of the columns in book form for easy access. One overenthusiastic reader even threatened my immortal soul, suggesting that I would be called to answer for my sins of omission at The Pearly Gates! Well, with enough to worry about on Judgment Day, I did not think that I could risk that.

And so I churned out the first book, *Ammo Grrrll Hits the Target*, to modest fanfare, a nice response, and some 52

5-Star Reviews on Amazon. My second book, *Ammo Grrrll Aims True*, was launched with a low-key campaign, barely mentioned within another column. Nobody likes a panderer…and yet, it has not sold as well as the first book where I nagged everyone I had ever known. There is a reason advertising – and nagging — actually work!

And now here comes Volume 3: *Ammo Grrrll Returns Fire*. Kids, this one is the best of all because this one covers the election run-up and the Righteous Red Meat Response to Hillary's famous "Deplorable" speech (p. 97). Hence, the title of the book. I believe that column alone is worth the price of the book. Oh, and Hillary will never be President. The 2016 election is covered on p.129. It never gets old.

I don't want to give away any more spoilers, so I will tell you that, if this is the 3rd book, and I am compiling a year's worth of columns into each book, there will be five books in all. Now, even with shipping and handling, when you buy all five, it would work out to cost roughly 33 cents a Friday column. I like to think that's a pretty decent bargain. You cannot buy a cup of coffee for that, even a Keurig cup. And that's paperback. E-book is pocket change.

Thank you. I am extremely grateful. Many of you say that I make YOU happy, and this whole enterprise makes me very happy. Happiness is what the left hates even more than success. As the Angel Clarence says in *It's a Wonderful Life*, "Every time you're happy or kind, a Leftist loses what's left of xer mind." At least I think that was it. Close enough.

DIY HATE CRIME HOAX KIT

March 1, 2019

It has come to my attention that my book sales — robust though they be — will simply not guarantee a comfortable retirement and I need to expand my product line.

What could be more timely or fill a better market niche in the current Hair Permanently On Fire Oppression Olympics than a Jussie Smollett Commemorative All-Purpose Do It Yourself Hate Crime Kit?

For the bargain-basement price of just $3500, you get:

- *Two sturdy Nigerians capable of delivering a carefully-calibrated beating;*
- *A rubber banana peel;*
- *One water-proof fake poop swastika with suction cup suitable for a dorm shower;*
- *Several lengths of rope, already fastened in nooses (for Scouts who were not in Scouting, back when you could earn a badge in knot-tying instead of Cooking with Tofu);*
- *A gallon of bleach which can also be used for laundry – WHITES ONLY (can I say that?);*
- *A dozen MAGA caps;*
- *One terrifying mask of a Catholic teenage white boy smiling;*
- *Fake dog poop in a tube of soothing crème suitable for self-smearing;*
- *One set of Sharpies in several colors and list of various offensive words – hurry!*

Unacceptable Words can change daily. Remember "macaca"? It actually influenced an election!

- *One traceable swastika stencil so you don't make it backwards like so many bigots with Carter era speed-limit IQ;*

- *A handy Velcro tear-away detachable hijab for easy removal;*

- *And a frozen Whole Foods cake with "Fag" pre-written on it so YOU, the gay Hate Crime Faker, don't have to waste valuable time or frosting writing that on your own.*

But wait, there's more! Because how can you fake a Hate Crime if you aren't even a member of a protected group that it's forbidden to hate? So act before midnight also to get:

- *A lovely set of High Cheekbone Implants;*

- *The Ward Churchill Detachable Braid with Eagle Feather Made in China;*

- *The Rachel Dolezal black fright wig.*

Nobody cares if white men or Conservative White Women (icky poo), Conservative Black People (even worse!) or (Gag) CHRISTIANS or weather-wizardy JOOZ are hated. They are attacked daily in the media and sometimes in person, though that carries risks. Remember: whatever happens to them, they have it coming. Because Trump. A woman lawyer (a LAWYER!) cheered the horrendous Las Vegas mass murder because the victims were country western fans and "most of them like guns and are Republican." Well, okay then.

And, FINALLY, as a SUPER SPECIAL BONUS, we will include a pair of Jimmy Choo Size 14EEE high heels in ecru

– they go with everything! This last item is not to stage a Hate Crime per se. No, it is to PREVENT one.

We purveyors of the Hate Crime Kit feel that if an enormous, unhinged, ugly, obviously male customer in an auto parts store is wearing high heels, it could lower the risk that he will be "gender misidentified" and called "Sir," thus causing a meltdown and kick-a-thon that would make a two-year-old jealous. In truth, he was neither a "Sir" nor a "Ma'am," which implies some sort of manners and self-respect, but a dangerous deranged thug.

Just a small point on this subject: as an enthusiastically-heterosexual female with a somewhat-deeper voice than many females, I have FREQUENTLY been called "Sir" on the telephone. Especially when I have had a chest cold. Even when I am making airline or hotel reservations for a person named "Susan". Which always makes me laugh, rather than kick over displays. Because I am not insane.

I have always figured that the poor front-line person is forced to choose between "Sir" and "Ma'am" and would prefer mistakenly to call a woman "Sir" than to call a man "Ma'am." I have recovered from each separate unforgivable outrage within several seconds, correcting the person as gently as possible to avoid his embarrassment. If it weren't necessary to make an accurate reservation, I wouldn't even bother to correct him.

So thank you for ordering my DIY Hate Crime Kit! Good luck with planning your own Hate Crime. Poor Jussie thought he had the "perfect" Hate Crime, which had even been rehearsed! Plus he had hundreds of willing media stooges and Tweeting celebrity accomplices – Cher, Cory, Kamala, Maxine, Jim Carrey – to the extent that a not-very-paranoid person could ALMOST think it was COORDINATED to coincide with the stupid "anti-lynching" legislation. Because, as you know, murder is, like, totally NOT currently illegal. Yeah, I know – crazy, right?

And despite every advantage, look what happened to Jussie. (Well, nothing so far…but you never know.) His story stunk to high heavens from day one. But he and his platoon of lawyers are stickin' to that story like Titanic survivors to a piece of driftwood. Maybe he's going for an Insanity Plea. So how can YOU improve?

Remember to go where there are no cameras, no busybodies videotaping everything on their cellphones, no eyewitnesses. Try not to stage it in a part of town that elderly Tea Party/MAGA people would never be visiting in broad daylight, let alone at night. Do NOT pretend they said "This is MAGA country" in either Portland, Berkeley, the South Side of Chicago, or the Upper West Side of New York. Now it's true that "Can you please direct me to the Holland Tunnel?" does not sound as threatening as "This is MAGA Country," but trust me, no Trump supporter ever said that to a random gay black person. Or any black person. Or anyone else. Ever.

Arrange to have yourself more severely injured than a little teeny cut below the eye on your pretty face. In fact, I recommend you sustain a small-caliber gunshot wound where it will not hit a vital organ, such as to the head. That lends some verisimilitude to the hate crime charge, believe me. There will be flowers and candles on the spot of the assault and Elton John will write a song for you. Go big or go home.

FIFTEEN MINUTES

March 9, 2019

When I read about the tragic fire that devastated Paradise, California, a few months ago, one of the most heart-breaking pieces of information was that the lucky escapees had all of 15 minutes to gather what they could and get out with their lives. Nearly 60 people didn't make it.

I looked around at my accumulated possessions of a lifetime and wondered what on earth I would elect to save.

First of all, having recently sustained a minor but extremely painful burn on my right ring finger from a bizarre incident with a teacup hot enough to burn through three layers of skin (the dermis, epidermis, and Santa Maria, I think), I would now be inclined just to GET OUT and not even push the 15 minutes.

But stipulating that I really did have the 15 minutes without risk, what was worth saving? Most of the irreplaceable items are heavy and awkward – 14 large, combination picture/scrapbooks with tons of family history, lovingly organized over years by a person of late, late middle age who may or may not have a slight case of OCD; the little glass dog my maternal grandfather won at the fair in 1883 when he was five; my large triple-matted framed picture of my boyfriend, Gary Cooper; the hand-typed, framed letter Daddy got from the Secretary of the Navy when he mustered out after World War II.

I only have four or five pieces of "real" jewelry, most of far greater sentimental value than major worth – a pretty bracelet Mr. AG gave me for our 15th wedding anniversary exactly half a lifetime ago, another nice gold bracelet he gave me for my 50th birthday, and a couple other baubles, including my gold wedding band for which we paid $27 in 1967. But unless I'm working out with weights, I usually have that on.

There is no clothing that would make the cut, though quite a few favorites that I would miss if they were gone. It takes a long time to get t-shirts and jeans tempered to the perfect level of softness. When the yellow bags come around from Disabled Vets asking for "old clothing," I just have to write them a check and explain that I am still wearing my old clothing. Depending on the weather, I might try to throw in my Navajo blanket jacket I bought in Santa Fe when I had not come prepared for the temperature at that elevation. It cost $300, weighs about 40 pounds, and will keep one warm to 30 below zero. Perfect for visiting relatives in Minnesota from late September to mid-May.

I have no silly overpriced shoes from Jimmy Choo, Jimmy Kimmel, or Jimmy Stewart. I have three or four nice pairs of cowgirl boots, but none that couldn't be replaced. Also no insanely-expensive handbags, just a $19.95 black leather fanny pack, always in fashion, goes with everything. Haha. I kid. I know it's awful and fairly screams either "Clueless Tourist" or "Geezer!" I just don't care. It holds my Driver's License, Carry Permit, guest passes to the Desert Botanical Garden, insurance cards, some nice fortune cookie fortunes, one Visa Card, a nail clippers, a lipstick, and a little cash.

Naturally, besides the fanny pack, it would be rather important to have the checkbook and a bunch of financial records and, of course, the cellphone and computer, or at least the memory stick.

What the heck to do about firearms and especially an EXTREMELY heavy accumulation of ammo from whence I got my name and column? The weapons themselves are pretty conveniently located for easy access and urgent egress. On television and sometimes in old cowboy movies, ammo that caught fire would start going off. I don't know if that is accurate or not, but I think it would probably be safe for looters to come back in the vicinity by 2025.

We probably have well over 1000 books, winnowed way down from the 5000 we had before the move to Arizona. Many are out of print now, of course, and almost all of my favorite authors have gone to that Algonquin Roundtable in the Sky. Yeah, of course, there are e-books. I have such a device, thanks to Mr. AG, but I really prefer holding an actual book and turning the pages. Habits of a lifetime die hard. So there's at least a couple of shelves of absolute favorites that I might try to shovel into the trunk of the car.

Mr. AG (the famous novelist, Max Cossack, with his FABULOUS second novel – "Zarah's Fire" — coming within days on Amazon), and I are both overly attached to "souvenirs," defined as pretty much anything that triggers a fond memory. A lifetime of fond memories produce several drawers, bins, closets and one storage locker full of stuff that must be saved. Forever. When we pass away, we have no doubt whatsoever that our son will engage the world's largest dump truck to haul it all away. He has to make room for his own collection of priceless Bobbleheads and Twins plastic cups.

Our only hope at preserving anything is to become famous enough that either the Smithsonian or one of the three colleges I attended decides to archive all my gun show t-shirts and travel journals ("Gotta love Maui. Oh, the smell of plumeria! Had outstanding Macadamia Nut Pie for breakfast…" "Israel is amazing! Especially the Israeli Breakfast Buffet!" "Amsterdam is quite the city – hookers in windows and bikes thrown into the canals and wonderful steak from Argentina.").

With insights like those, preservation for posterity seems unlikely.

THE HAPPIEST PEOPLE IN THE WORLD

March 15, 2019

Ignorance, it has been said, is bliss. In which case you would surely guess that the Democrats and the congressional freshman twit class in particular would be the happiest people in the world. But you would be wrong. No, they are not happy; they are filled with venom, hatred, envy, resentment, and bizarre endless, self-generated rage. How tedious and depressing it must be to live with one of them!

One of the problems with living long (and prospering), is that one has seen it all before. Why, I was but a misguided young lass speaking at an anti-war rally at the University of Minnesota after the 1970 Kent State shootings when a disheveled young man no one had ever seen before on campus rushed the stage, grabbed my microphone, and screamed, "They're building concentration camps in California!" This was when college students were sturdier than today's crop, so there were a few shrieks of alarm and then the kids went back either to studying for finals or trying to score with that long-haired person of either sex next to them.

Ah, yes. Nixon was Hitler. As several have pointed out previously, not too long after that, Reagan was definitely Hitler and, then, at last the loons got a name with an "H" in it, so they could append "itler" onto George W. Bush's name. I was by that time, "transitioning" from a moderate Democrat to a conservative, but even I thought "Bushitler" was a mind-numbingly stupid and wildly-inaccurate nickname. Especially for what seemed – even when I disagreed with him politically – to be a nice and sincere gentleman, if anything TOO nice and entirely unwilling to defend himself or, by extension, those of us who supported him. And yet Bushitler appeared on hundreds of signs for 8 years.

But, while those previous pikers were "kinda sorta Hitlerish," it took the acumen of the ironically-named Joy Behar to suss out the truth that Donald J. Trump was "LITERALLY" Hitler. No pale orange imitation he but the real deal. Of course, she also said that Trump's collusion with Putin meant we would soon see the Russian flag flying above the Stars and Stripes over the White House, so consistency, or even lucidity, is not her long suit.

But how did the rest of us – especially the JOOZ who voted for him! – miss such obvious similarities between Hitler and Donald J. Trump? When it was clear that:

Hitler killed either "several" Jews (according to Arab sources) or 6 million Jews (according to the Nazis' own meticulous records). Donald J. Trump has killed no one. Ever.

Hitler was a vegetarian – DJT puts ketchup on his steak.

Hitler died a virgin – whatever else happens to DJT, that will not be happening.

No German media outlet dared to criticize Hitler – no American media outlet dares to say a single mumblin' positive word about DJT lest they appear to "normalize" him.

I could go on.

Another endlessly recycled scary scenario is to suggest that whatever Bad Fascist Republican President is in office that he will not leave when he loses the next election or his two legal terms are up. This was suggested most recently by Juan Williams, who I have always said seems like the sweetest person to be wrong about "literally" EVERYTHING.

The old and still sometimes funny SNL did a skit during Reagan's term wherein Nancy had to be hauled kicking and screaming from the White House. It goes without saying that Bushitler was not going to leave. Oopsie. He was unusually gracious in showing the Obama family the ropes in the White House and reportedly he and Michelle remain close friends.

It was political savant and actress Gwyneth Paltrow who gushed to Obama her wish that he could be President for Life, (a la Papa Doc Duvalier, Fidel Castro, or Fatty Un) because – wait for it – he was just so gosh-darned good-looking. Oh, my.

Speaking of actresses, Debra Messing – Mr. AG had to tell me who she was; that's okay, she's never heard of me, either – stirred up a Twitter storm when she baked Vagina Cupcakes for International Women's Day, March 8th, and then had to fall on her sword or rolling pin or whatever because NOT ALL WOMEN HAVE VAGINAS!

Let us not dwell overlong on what the Vagina Cupcakes looked like, complete with sprinkles to represent hair, lest I never eat another cupcake again. (Personally, I might have just gone with the Vagina Donut.) But the point is that she was forced to grovel for the grave sin of failing to pretend that men who haven't even gone to the trouble of mutilating themselves can still be women.

She said she meant no offense and intended the treats to be "sassy." There will BE no "sassy" in the New World Order, luv, nor any kind of fun. Remember Afghanistan where you could be punished for kite-flying? (Jerry Seinfeld: "evidently the Taliban were afraid someone would discover electricity…") (AG: has Venezuela thought of kites?)

And so I repeat my oft-offered mantra: in times like these, it is a revolutionary act to laugh in the face of the lynch mob;

happiness is not only a goal, but a weapon. Of course, it is no substitute for an ACTUAL weapon, and I heartily encourage you to own several, but it is a potent weapon nonetheless.

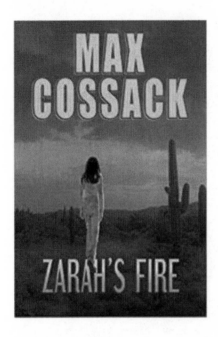

Want to buy some Instant Happiness? Order Max Cossack's terrific new book — *Zarah's Fire* — off Amazon and curl up in bed with your cat, dog or sweetie. Wait for the book to arrive. Something will probably occur to you while you wait. More happiness! If you are a Prime member, it could be a short wait for the paperback or no wait at all for an e-book.

STUPID AND DANGEROUS RULES FOR GIRLS

March 22, 2019

The awesome Heather Mac Donald had her usual brilliant take a few weeks ago on Joni Ernst's disappointing objections to Neomi Rao's judicial confirmation based on her college writing about what women can and should do to protect themselves from sexual assault.

As I understand Senator Ernst's objections, the new rule is: Under no circumstances should girls and women EVER have to assume any responsibility for decisions that could adversely affect them. NOTHING is girls' and women's fault. EVER. GOT THAT?

There is no such thing as women actually in charge of either their decision-making or their appearance or their bodies in general. There is only toxic masculinity (Def.: ANY masculinity), and an entire pathetic sex of helpless victims. We have come full circle from the Victorian fainting couch with a brief pit stop in the "I am woman, hear me roar" and Xena Warrior period to the current need for a Safe Room, Play-Doh, and Twitter Mob to make sure nobody dares to step out of line.

If that Twitter Mob can make a tough and righteous icon like Martina Navratilova "apologize" for stating the obvious fact that men pretending to be women are going to win every athletic contest with actual women, then who among us dares to question?

Further, there is no statute of limitations on the fall-out from any bad decisions. Girls who had drunk sex in, say, 1962, can go in front of television cameras with a fleet of sleazy lawyers in 2019 and cry about what happened and name names – or even make them up! — and every male named by 50-year-old memories or fabrications will be called in the press "credibly accused." Unless the males are Democrat, black, Muslim, or any combination of these things. On the Intersectional Scorecard, more is always better.

Did your Mama or some old busybody candidate for a judgeship (back when she was in college) advise you not to get black-out drunk when you are on a date? Well, what do THEY know? You do not need to be careful at all. It is really empowering to drink till you throw up in your purse. Which actually happened to a guy friend of mine on a first date. There wasn't a second date…and oddly enough, he didn't feel like having sex, forced or consensual, with a vomiting woman. But rest assured, ladies, whatever ensues after that will in no way be any part of your fault. That's the key takeaway lesson here: you are not responsible.

As a cis-normal, heterosexual woman of the female persuasion who identifies as a free adult, I am so appalled by the notion that we cannot decrease our chances of a bad sexual outcome by our smart and responsible behavior that I need a "comfort item," possibly a .45.

Are people too stupid to live? Do not go into a hardcore biker bar in a Hooters-style outfit unless you want to attract attention. What other reason would there even BE for wearing that outfit? If you do want to attract attention, fine. Own it. Does it mean that you "deserve" to be groped or, God forbid, assaulted? Of course not, and those things happen to be illegal. But, seriously, why are you there wearing that outfit? Are you looking for a "boyfriend"? Do any of these guys look like husband material to you?

See, women talking amongst themselves recognize reality and even celebrate it. Almost every woman in America has a pair of sexy high heels she and her girlfriends refer to candidly as "_____ me" shoes. When being honest, women know absolutely that some outfits have predictable consequences. Which is precisely why they buy and wear them!

Does that mean that you are "asking for it"? Well, that depends on whether or not you were. In almost any major city, you can find women wearing ridiculous clothing like fishnet stockings, leather boots, a loin-cloth length skirt, and a low-cut top. They stand on street corners advertising their bodies for sale. In fact, that outfit is so iconic as "asking for it" indeed, "soliciting" for it, that it is often used as an adorable Hallowe'en costume at adult parties. So, if YOU look like a hooker, you are going to send a "mixed" message. At best.

Here's some more unwanted and unwelcome advice:

Do not go to a man's hotel room, even to "get some papers" or "see what's in the mini-bar" or any other pretend reason. A hotel room is actually a bedroom. If you go there, men will assume you know that and have agreed to do one of the two things most people do in bedrooms. One of them is sleep. Do you think the man who has convinced you to go to his room just wants a little nap?

There is no doubt that Bill Cosby is one sick creepy puppy. Here was a television icon, JELLO spokesman, groundbreaking black actor, rich as Croesus, who either could have paid professionals like Tiger Woods did, or could have convinced any number of women to "date" him. He also had a stunningly-beautiful wife. But evidently what jerked his bobber was to drug and assault comatose women. Yikes! Now, the sheer number of accusers was certainly daunting. From my observation on #MeToo in all its forms, and what I know about people who love to hop on the victim bandwagon, especially if there's a lucrative payday, I'm going to guess that a certain percentage of his accusers are lying. But what of the others, some of whom tried to press charges decades earlier?

Almost every case where details were released involved the accuser being alone with this icky married man – either in a hotel room or in his own home with the wife nowhere in sight! – often allegedly in search of "help" with or "advice" on the woman's potential career. And, oh yeah, always with alcohol involved.

The popular feminist trope that women comics were somehow "held down" by powerful men is the usual poppycock peddled by the talentless and the envious. I got lots of help from men in my comedy career. We met in restaurants and offices. There was neither "hanky" nor "panky," although club owner Dudley Riggs (now in his 90s, bless him) did once offer me his clean white hanky to mop my brow when we had extremely hot Sri Lankan curry in a restaurant. Does anyone have Gloria Allred's cell? Maybe there's still a chance that that was some kind of micro-aggression. A WHITE hanky? Clear dog whistle.

THE COLUMN TURNS FIVE!

March 29, 2019

Historically, March has always meant St. Patrick's Day, depressing hockey-tournament blizzards in Minnesota just when you thought winter was ending, and the NCAA March Madness tournaments. And now the world must add: the anniversary of my "Thoughts From the Ammo Line" column on Power Line! And this anniversary is a special one. For whatever reason, we seem to get especially enthused about anniversaries and birthdays that end in "5" or "0".

At this stage of life, I am just as pleased to live to an age ending in "1" or "9" or anything in between. A dear friend dealing with an extremely ill but resilient kitty cat welcomed us to her home the other night. She pointed in sweeping Vanna style to the plucky, comeback cat sitting on the couch and said, "Look who's still alive!" I suggested that as our late, late middle-aged friendship group ages, that should be the central theme of all of our gatherings. I'm designing cocktail napkins with that sentiment on them.

For four straight years, I have reprised the story of how I came to be standing in ammo lines and then how I got the column. I am tired of telling it; it is featured at the beginning of all three of my column-compilations, *Ammo Grrrll Hits the Target, Ammo Grrrll Aims True,* and *Ammo Grrrll Returns Fire*. Buy one, two, or all of them. Nothing says "Happy Anniversary, Ammo Grrrll," like a 5-Star Review on Amazon and the massive $6.00 profit I make off each book! Woohoo! Starbucks' Iced Caramel Macchiato for me (small size) tomorrow! Thank you.

To celebrate my 5th anniversary, The Worst Hitler Ever recognized Israel's sovereignty over the Golan Heights. And something else happened that I can't quite recall since it was several days ago:

Oh, yeah, it's coming back to me now – the Mueller report concluded that President Trump is not a Russian agent and there was NO COLLUSION with Putin to snatch the election from the rightful greedy grasping hands of Hillary Clinton. She managed to blow that lock of a predicted landslide election all by her lonesome! It's almost as if the losing loser who called ME a Deplorable lost twice. Or three times, counting her loss to Barack Hussein Obama. Four, if you count her marriage to Bill "Cigar Boy" Clinton. I could go on…

As if that weren't enough to make me dance like no one was watching, Creepy Porn Lawyer, CNN Super-Star, and Democrat Presidential timber Michael Avenatti was arrested both for extorting Nike and for stealing money from clients. Can it get any better than that?

Well, yes, it can. For frosting on a Death by Chocolate Cake, Rachel Maddow cried because her President is not a Russian agent. Suh-weet! Suck it up, Buttercup!

John Brennan – who looks like the spawn of Helen Thomas and Satan (they dated in high school) – is going to need some kind of Brillo pad and Lava soap even to begin to wash all the egg off his face. And, of course, he is not alone. Dried egg all round.

But the Spin Doctors and Lying Liars Who Lie have been working feverishly for several days. Two main themes have emerged from the leftist losers on the losing side: ONE: "Hey, what about the obstruction?" and TWO: "The media did a super-duper, bang-up job of covering this two-year debacle." The really deranged add, "Mueller must also be a compromised Russian agent. It goes without saying that Barr is." Oh my.

I watched my new (imperfect, wrong on immigration) hero, Lindsey Graham, star of the Kavanaugh hearings, in a terrific news conference. He gave fair warning that "now it's our turn." When it came time for the Q and A, not one trained seal in the press corps addressed a single thing he had spoken about. The first THREE tedious, repetitive questions were all about "obstruction" and I left the room.

Word of the day is now "obstruction" instead of "collusion," which the New Urban Dictionary now defines as: "THAT didn't work; please try again." And, please, for the sake of our collective sanity, give these brain-dead babbling bimbos of both sexes a new catchphrase for "Is this the beginning of the end?" You can YouTube those words and find President Trump has been at the beginning of the end since he came down that escalator, maybe since birth. You would think SOMEBODY would be embarrassed. But you would be wrong. There is no shame; there is no apology; there is no learning; there is no bottom.

Finally, as if we needed any more evidence that there is no bottom, the one icky item floating in the punchbowl in an otherwise wonderful day came out of Chicago. Jussie Smollett is still sticking by his ludicrous story of being attacked by MAGA hat white men and the justice system in the banana republic of Chicago has dropped all charges against him for the obvious hoax. In the stirring words of the late Johnnie Cochran: "If it doesn't fit, you must acquit." We're also told that everything is "sealed." Well, heck, that ain't no thang. All the divorce records of both of Obama's opponents were "sealed" too, and yet they became unsealed within plenty of time to benefit the Lightbringer. Get him on the case.

I honestly hope Jussie never works again and is driven from the public square, but I have lived long enough to know that he will be just fine. His network even gloated that he has been "vindicated." Oh boy.

Finally, as I do every year at this time, I would like to thank the Power Line boys who extend me my platform every Friday. And express my eternal gratitude to the many smart, fascinating and encouraging readers and commenters it has been my privilege to get to know through the column. Among them: a sports team owner, an astronaut in Oregon, a poet in Connecticut, a libertarian rancher in Montana who buys my books in bulk to give away like Gideon Bibles, a retired sheriff from Alabama (Roll, Tide), and a father of 6 from Massachusetts who sings in a Barbershop Quartet and is working on a book of children's stories about the IDF. Am I a lucky Grrrll, or what?

AFTERWORD

If someone had told me when I sent Scott Johnson that first brief reflection on my new interest in self-defense and target-shooting, that I would still be cranking out regular columns five years later, I would have been both delighted and terrified. Sometimes, Life is more unpredictable than Mr. Toad's Wild Ride, which, if memory serves me, is only slightly "wilder" than the Small, Small World snooze-fest. Mr. Toad was not exactly a Navy Seal.

But, as long as I have cranked out some 250 opinion pieces – probably about three months' output for each of my Power Line colleagues – I figure to keep plugging until they don't want me anymore. I still feel strongly about the ceaseless war for the culture, for Western Civilization, for the heart and soul of this great country, and I don't want to abandon my post. If I have nothing new or important to say on a given Friday, perhaps I can at least help with the morale of someone who does.

My initial mission was to help Scott, my editor, with his anger management problem. Like every mission in history, there has been some "mission creep", but I still remain committed to that original goal.

So, look for Book Six, "Ammo Grrrll Reloads", covering the period from March of 2019 to March of 2020, probably making its appearance sometime in April or May of 2020.

God Bless America. Our Republic – Let's Keep It!

Susan Vass
November 30, 2019

Made in the USA
San Bernardino, CA
24 January 2020